SHARING NATURE WITH CHILDREN

by Joseph Bharat Cornell

Edited by George Beinhorn

A Parents' and Teachers' Nature–Handbook

Contents

Introduction

Activities

Appendices

© Joseph Bharat Cornell
Published by Exley Publications Limited,
12 Ye Corner, Watford, Herts, UK WD1 4BS.
ISBN 0 905521 36 6 (hardcover)
ISBN 0 905521 37 4 (paperback)
Original edition published in January 1979
by Ananda Publications, California, USA
Printed by Dainippon Tien Wah Printing (PTE)
Limited, 977 Bukit Timah Road, Singapore 21.

TO
*Those who experience
nature's inspiring, transforming
moments, and who desire to share with others,
their love for the natural world.*

AND
*S.K., who by simply living his life,
has given me a greater
understanding of my own.*

Introduction

WHEN 'Sharing Nature with Children' first appeared in the United States, it was published in a very limited edition by Ananda Publications, a small publishing co-operative on the West Coast. But almost immediately the intrinsic value of the book caught people's attention. The Scouts, the conservation societies, the press, parents — all were struck by Joseph Bharat Cornell's sensitive and imaginative ideas for introducing children to the world of nature.

Within months, and without high pressure salesmanship, sales of the book rocketed and Scout and youth organisations all over the continent began adopting Joseph's ideas.

For years Joseph Cornell had had a growing influence on conservation and nature teaching. He had been (and still is) running workshops for group leaders and parents. Many experts have come to his workshops time and again to share his knowledge and enthusiasm.

"Our staff were taken by Joseph's naturalness and love for the earth," said one naturalist, from America's leading conservation group. "When he was outdoors, it was obvious that Joseph was in his element. He had a childlike quality, and it always seemed to him the earth was a place of beauty and mystery. He loved to work with children, and his uninhibited joyfulness allowed children to be themselves around him: to play Indians in the tall grass, to climb a tree, to do all those things children love doing. And while he played with them, Joseph always promoted perception and sensitivity towards the earth."

In today's world of overpopulation and high consumption, it is essential that we make an effort to keep children in touch with the earth: its natural rhythms, the changing seasons, its beauty and mystery. In fact, nothing will suffice, short of teaching children to love nature, to love life.

Rachel Carson, in her book, *The Sense of Wonder,* claimed that, when introducing a child to the excitement of the natural world, "It is not half so important to *know* as to *feel*." It is in this spirit that Joseph has written this book — as an aid to parents and youth leaders in helping children to become more aware of the world around them, and to help them know the deep personal satisfaction of being in touch with the earth.

THE UNUTTERABLE BEAUTY of a blossom. The grace of a high-flying bird. The roar of wind in the trees: at one time or another in our lives, nature touches you, and me . . . and all of us in some personal special way. Her immense mystery opens up to us with stunning purity, reminding us of a life that is greater than the little affairs of man.

I have never underestimated the value of such moments of touching and entering into nature. I have seen through my own experience and that of many others, that we can nourish that deeper awareness until it becomes a true and vital understanding of our place in this world.

I collected and developed the games in this book during years of working with children as a nature-awareness instructor. I wanted to help children to be inspired by nature; Mother Nature's lessons are especially valuable for the growing child. And so that is what this book is all about: using nature to stimulate joyful, enlightening insights and experiences — for ourselves, as well as for our children and child-friends.

Some people have scientific, logical minds, while others are more sensitively attuned to beauty and harmony; and still others are moved most deeply by the eternal philosophical truths. The forty-two games presented in this book will open up nature to children — and adults — of all temperaments. Each of the games creates a situation, or an experience, in which nature is the teacher. Each game is a mouthpiece for nature — sometimes speaking in the language of the scientist, sometimes in that of the artist or mystic.

Preface

The first group of games brings us into harmony with our natural surroundings on the physical and emotional level. Later on there are games that create a quiet, contemplative mood. (Don't think for a minute that the "quiet" games are boring; I've seen players experience such calm, intense alertness that their memories of the games stayed with them for years, giving fresh inspiration every time those memories were brought to mind.)

Some of the games give us an inside view of the way nature works — the principles of ecological systems, for example — but not in a boring, textbook way. While we play the games, we act out dynamically, and feel directly, the natural cycles and processes. Children understand and remember concepts best when they learn from direct personal experience.

Still other games tune our finer feelings to the special qualities of the nature world — peace and beauty; energy and grandeur; mystery and wonder. We communicate with nature directly by touch, smell, taste, sight, and sound.

Some of the games are purely fun. The natural exuberance of childhood is in its element in the woods or in tall grass, or under a starlit summer sky. As adults, we cherish our memories of such childhood scenes, because they touch something deep inside us.

I happily offer these nature-awareness games to you and your child-friends. Use them sensitively and with joy and you're sure to experience a beautiful new attunement and exchange of energy with nature's intelligence and goodness.   *Joseph Cornell*

Sharing your Love of Nature

(A Few Suggestions for Good Teaching)

BEFORE WE BEGIN exploring nature with children, let's think for a moment about our role as teachers or leaders. What are the basic rules for giving children — and ourselves — a joyful, rewarding good time? I would like to share with you five tenets of outdoor teaching that have helped me work with energetic, lively children — channelling them away from mischief towards more constructive, and ultimately satisfying, pursuits. Underlying these principles are basic attitudes of respect for children and reverence for nature — attitudes to which they will surely respond.

1. Teach less, and share more. Besides telling children the bare facts of nature ("This is a mountain hemlock tree."), I like to tell them about my inner feelings in the presence of that tree. I tell them about my awe and respect for the way a hemlock can survive in subalpine conditions — where water is scarce in summer, and mostly frozen in winter; where harsh winter winds twist and bend and kill its branches. And I tell them I always wonder how the roots of the hemlock ever manage to find enough nutrients to survive, in these solid-rock crevices.

Children respond to my observations much more freely than they respond to textbook explanations. Take the case of a hemlock tree that grew near a camp where I worked. This particular hemlock sits between two huge boulders, so it has had to send its roots down twenty-five feet to reach the stony soil below. At the time, it was at least two hundred years old, and only eight feet tall. The children would frequently make a detour on their walks just to empty their water bottles at its roots. Several of them returned to the camp year after year, watching the tree's stubborn struggle for life in its harsh environment. In fact, as soon as they arrived at camp, they would run out to see how it had fared through the dry autumn and cold winter. Their loving concern awakened in me an even deeper respect for the mountain hemlock.

I believe it is important for an adult to share his inner self with a child. Only by sharing our deeper thoughts and feelings do we communicate to, and inspire in others, a love and respect for the earth. When we share our own ideas, it encourages a child to explore his own feelings and perceptions. A wonderful mutual trust and friendship develops between the adult and the child.

2. Be receptive. Receptivity means listening and being aware. It is one of the most richly rewarding attitudes you can cultivate while working with children. The outdoors brings out a spontaneous enthusiasm in the child that you can skilfully direct towards learning.

Be sensitive: every question, every comment, every joyful exclamation is an opportunity to communicate. Respond to the child's present mood and feelings. Expand your child's interests by teaching along the grain of his own curiosity. You'll always find that when you respect his thoughts, your time with him will flow easily and happily.

Be alert also to what nature is doing around you at the present moment. Something exciting or interesting is almost always happening. Your lesson plan will be written for you minute by minute if you tune in with sensitive attention.

3. Focus the child's attention without delay. Set the tone of the outing right at the start. Involve everyone as much as you can, by asking questions and pointing out interesting sights and sounds. Some children are not used to watching nature closely, so find things that interest them, and lead them bit by bit into the spirit of keen observation. Let them feel that their findings are interesting to you, too.

4. Look and experience first; talk later. At times nature's spectacles will seize the child in rapt attention: a newly-emerged dragonfly pumping fluid into tender unfolding wings, a lone deer grazing in a forest clearing. But even if those special sights are lacking, the child can have an experience of wonder by just watching quite ordinary things with close attention. Children have a marvellous capacity for absorbing themselves in whatever they're looking at. Your child will gain a far better understanding of things outside himself by becoming one with them than he will from second-hand facts. Children seldom forget a direct experience.

Don't worry about not knowing names. The names of plants and animals are only superficial labels for what those things really *are*. Just as your own essence isn't captured by your name, or even by your physical and personality traits, there is also much more to an oak tree, for example, than a name and a list of facts about it. You can gain a deeper appreciation of an oak tree by watching how the tree's mood shifts with changes in lighting at different times of day. Observe the tree from unusual perspectives. Feel and smell its bark and leaves. Quietly sit on or under its branches, and be aware of all the forms of life that live in and around the tree and depend on it.

Look. Ask questions. Guess. Have fun! As your children begin to develop an empathy with nature, your relationship with them will evolve from one of teacher and fellow-student to one of fellow-adventurer.

5. *A sense of joy should permeate the experience,* whether in the form of gaiety or calm attentiveness. Children are naturally drawn to learning if you can keep the spirit of the occasion happy and enthusiastic. Remember that your own enthusiasm is infectious, and that it is perhaps your greatest asset as a teacher.

Choosing the Right Game for the Time and Place

THE NATURE GAMES in this book will teach children many kinds of lessons — some obvious, some quite subtle. You may want to use certain games because of the personal qualities they develop in the child, or because of the concepts they teach. You can also choose games to complement the mood of your group, or to create a desirable change in attitude or energy. To make it easy for you to tell quickly what each game is like, I have included with each activity a quick-reference box, like the one on the opposite page.

A. Basic mood of each game is indicated by one of three animal symbols:

Calm/Reflective
Deer harm nobody. They are very shy but left to themselves they rest calmly during the day and graze quietly at dawn and dusk.

Active/Observational
The crow is an extremely alert and intelligent rascal, who's likely to be found keenly observing anything that's going on.

Energetic/Playful
The otter spends his days frolicking; the only animal that plays (constantly!) throughout adult life, he is nature's embodiment of exuberant fun.

B. What the child will learn
C. When and where to play
D. Number of players needed
E. Best age range
F. Special materials needed, if any

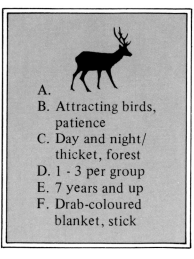

A.
B. Attracting birds, patience
C. Day and night/ thicket, forest
D. 1 - 3 per group
E. 7 years and up
F. Drab-coloured blanket, stick

A CLOSE TO NATURE

few years ago, a naturalist at an outdoor education camp led a group of children on a very special hike. I was a participant rather than a leader that day, and I still enjoy my memories of the outing. Our leader created dramatic, contrasting experiences for us that ensured that all of us would have deep, new, personal contacts with the natural world.

Most of the children had never been in an evergreen forest in their lives, and we were going to a rather rare pine forest. (This forest of pines was planted many years ago as part of an arboretum, a place where trees are scientifically studied.) The children were excited, and our naturalist-guide channelled their high energy skilfully to create a moving experience of the forest.

She first took us to a Christmas-tree farm, where she announced with a flourishing sweep of an arm and a twinkle in her eye, "This is the pine forest." Groans and disappointed shuffling of feet — the trees were barely taller than the children.

She then blindfolded all of us and led us through a sunny deciduous forest. Pretty soon we heard a stream and she said, "There's a narrow bridge here, so you'll have to cross one at a time." The first child started across, then shrieked with nervous laughter. The rest of us waited uneasily, not knowing what was ahead.

My turn came and I groped my way forward, taking a first cautious step onto the bridge. Aha! No wonder there were squeals — the bridge swayed dizzily from side to side, and bounced up and down at the same time. Between the creaks and groans of ropes and wood, I heard water rushing along far below. At the other side I was greeted by a flutter of small hands; the naturalist had let the children take off their blindfolds to watch me cross. I now removed my own blindfold and saw a safely-built suspension bridge, its handrails polished from much use.

We replaced our blindfolds and struck out on

the trail again. After a while the sound of our footsteps changed; we heard no more crackling leaves, only a soft, muffled crunching as we walked. Then there was a dark shadow all around us and we sensed a deep quiet — fewer bird sounds, and no rustling of leaves in the wind. A child broke the silence: "Where are we?"

The naturalist said, "Lie down on your backs and try to feel what is special about this place."

We lay for a long time experiencing the deep, restful quiet. Finally, the naturalist told us to take off our blindfolds. Shooting skywards were countless magnificent pine trees. My spirits rose with them, and I was overwhelmed with admiration and awe — I had never seen a forest this way before. The children were completely stunned. Finally, we sat up and looked around at each other, quietly sharing our amazement. On our own we wandered through the forest, touching the trees and gazing up into the forest cathedral.

It takes a happy combination of setting and receptivity to have a really deep experience like this. That's what the games in this chapter are for: to bring us that fresh and mysterious contact with other members of the natural world about us.

A.
B. Appreciating nature, calmness
C. Day/forest floor
D. 1 or more
E. 7 years and up
F. None

THE FOREST looks fresh and interesting, when you see it from a brand-new angle. In this game, the children lie still on the forest floor, absorbed in watching and listening to swaying trees, fluttering birds, and the rushing wind. Through holes in its leafy ceiling, silent clouds peek into the children's woodsy room. Animals may come very close because the children are quiet and hidden.

Ask everyone to lie down, to look skywards and to begin thinking of themselves as part of the earth. Cover each child's body with leaves, sticks and pine needles — right up to the sides of the head. Leave only the face exposed, and use enough leaves and sticks to give a feeling of being down inside the earth. Now place leaves (pine needles work best) over the children's faces, patchwork-fashion. Make sure the leaves are free of dirt, and tell the children to close their eyes as you arrange this final bit of covering.

Tell the children you'll give a signal when it's time to come back; this will help them stay under the leaves longer without getting restless. You should give the signal before they become restless. Surprisingly, I've found that twenty minutes is usually not too long.

In a large group, work quickly and let the children help bury each other. Work in one direction, away from those covered first. Then when the first-covered emerge, you can steer them away from the others who are still enjoying the forest quiet. Any individuals or pairs who are likely to talk and disturb those around them can be buried some distance away from the others.

Children will be much more agreeable to the idea of being covered with soil and leaves if they've been digging or crawling on the forest floor just before the game begins. It's important also to say something in advance about the bugs that may crawl over them. Play this down! You may want to let the children first handle various bugs, allowing the bugs to crawl over them. This is often a lot of fun — the children lose their early-learned pre-judices against insects, and begin to appreciate these fascinating little creatures. Encourage them to stay calm while lying under the leaves and being crawled upon; ask them just to feel what the bug is doing, so that they can tell the others about it afterwards.

Earth Windows gives an experience of the forest through the forest's own eyes.

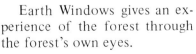

Earth Windows

A

TREE is a living crea-
ture. It eats, rests, breathes and circulates its
"blood" much as we do. The heartbeat of a tree
is a wonderful crackling, gurgling flow of life.
The best time to hear the forest heartbeat is in
early spring, when the trees send first surges of sap
upward to their branches, preparing them for another season of growth.

Choose a tree that is at least six inches in diameter
and has thin bark. Deciduous trees are generally

Heartbeat

A.
B. Appreciating nature,
   tree physiology
C. Day/wood
D. 1 or more
E. 4 years and up
F. Stethoscope

better for listening to than conifers, and certain individuals of a species may have a louder heartbeat than others. Press a stethoscope firmly against the tree, keeping it motionless so as not to make interfering noises. You may have to try several different places on the tree trunk before you find a good listening spot.

Children will want to hear their own heartbeat. Listen also to the heartbeats of mammals and birds — the variety in sounds and rhythms is fascinating.

# of a Tree

An Introduction to Blindfold Activities

THE GAMES in this section stimulate children's imaginations as perhaps no other games in this book can.

Blindfold activities dislodge our thoughts from self-preoccupation, and free our awareness to embrace more of the world around us. Vision is the sense we depend on most. Deprived of sight, we must fall back on our less-used senses of hearing, touch, and smell. Our attention is powerfully focused on these senses, and our perceptions through them are intensified. The babbling of our minds slows down, overwhelmed by the information that our fully-awake senses are giving us.

I vividly remember my first blindfold experience. I was led down a path to a stream, which I entered up to my knees, splashing around and feeling the current. My guide asked me if I'd like to float downstream. Well, in we went! At first we floated cautiously, but soon I was able to relax and give myself to the current, drifting along wherever it led. I was delighted by the crosscurrents that turned and twisted my body, while gurglings, roarings, swishings and bubblings composed the most wonderful music. I had never known a stream to be such a marvellous thing!

(Caution: Unless you and your guide are familiar with the particular stream, and water safety procedures, it would be best to start your blind experiences with one of the activities in this chapter.)

A.
B. Using smell and touch, trust
C. Day/anywhere
D. 2 or more
E. 3 years and up
F. Blindfolds

Blind Walk

IT'S VERY SIMPLE to organize and lead a blind walk. Form pairs, with mixed adults and children, or children together. Each pair decides who'll be the leader first, and who'll be blindfolded. The leader guides his partner along any route that looks attractive — being very careful to watch out for logs, low branches, and so on. The leader also guides his blind partner's hands to interesting objects, and brings him within range of interesting sounds and smells.

Meet a Tree

A.
B. Using smell and touch
C. Day/forest
D. 2 or more
E. 4 years and up
F. Blindfolds

THIS GAME is for groups of at least two. Pair off. Blindfold your partner and lead him through the forest to any tree that attracts you. (How far will depend on your partner's age and ability to orientate himself. For all but very young children, a distance of 20-30 yards usually isn't too far.)

Help the "blind" child to explore his tree and to feel its uniqueness. I find that specific suggestions are best. For example, if you tell children to *"Feel the tree"*, they won't respond with as much interest as if you say *"Rub your cheek on the bark."* Instead of *"Explore your tree,"* be specific: *"Is this tree still alive? . . . Can you put your arms around it? . . . Is the tree older than you are? . . . Can you find plants growing on it? . . . Animal signs? . . . Lichens. . . . Insects?"*

When your partner has finished exploring, lead him back to where you began, but take an indirect route. (This part of the game has its fun side, with the guides leading their partners over imaginary logs and through thickets that might easily have been avoided.) Now, remove the blindfold and let the child try to find the tree with his eyes open. Suddenly, as the child searches for *his* tree, what was a forest becomes a collection of very individual trees.

A tree can be an unforgettable experience in the child's life. Often children have come back to me a year after we played Meet a Tree, and have literally dragged me out to the forest to say, "Look! Here's my tree!"

A.
B. Developing smell and touch, trust
C. Day/anywhere
D. 1 or more
E. 5 years and up
F. Rope, blindfolds

Blindfold Trail

ON A BLINDFOLD Trail a rope-guided group of travellers roam through lands full of strange sounds, mysterious smells, and interesting textures. Most travellers can hardly wait to retrace their steps through this enchanted land with eyes open.

To make your trail exciting, find an area that offers a variety of experiences. An example of a good Blindfold Trail might be: follow a shady wooded path climb over a moss-covered log; emerge into a sunlit clearing humming with summer bees, dive again into the forest (this time crawling beneath a dense canopy of six-foot pine saplings), and feel and hear the smooth, dry needles crackle under your hands and knees. The smell of damp vegetation and a chorus of startled ducks announce your arrival at what can only be a pond.

A really good Blindfold Trail takes a fair amount of time to set up; but even a quickly-improvised one can be worthwhile. The important elements to keep in mind are: variety, theme, and mystery. For example, you can create a varied experience of touch, hearing, and smell; or arrange for contrasts within one sense — a rough and a smooth rock; tender new leaves and dry, crackly, dead ones; or a rich, moist odour and a sweet spring fragrance. (Tie a knot in the line to indicate that there's an interesting smell nearby.) Another way to add variety is to make the rope go up and down by attaching it to interesting objects on the ground and overhead.

A specific theme helps to link the various experiences together in the children's minds, especially if you tell them that there will be a special theme. Some possible themes are: tree identification, exploring an animal habitat; or contrasting local climates. (A local climate is a well-defined area — like the sun-shaded north side of a hill — with its own unique conditions of temperature, moisture, and vegetation.) It's easy to include an element of mystery: anything unfamiliar is mysterious. For instance, a string leading away from the main line and descending into a deep hole in a tree is a very good mystery experience.

Before laying out the trail, decide which side of the rope the children will walk on. (Be sure to tell them to stay on that side.) Keep safety in mind and make sure there aren't any poisonous plants in the area.

A calm, receptive mind greatly enhances the child's enjoyment of the trail, so it's very helpful to precede the Blindfold Trail experience with a story or some other quiet activity. Before you start the game, you might guide the children's hands over a tree trunk. Ask them to hug the tree and guess how big it is, and how it feels. Offer them a leaf to smell. Give them some idea of how to explore the trail, so they won't just run through it. Encourage them to be silent as they explore.

The Blindfold Trail is one of my favourite games. It develops the spirit of receptivity that is needed for every kind of nature experience.

A.
B. Concentration,
   imitation
C. Day and night/
   anywhere
D. 1 or more
E. 4 years and up
F. None

Role-Playing

BE A DANDELION PARACHUTE, freely drifting. Or a tree; feel your highest branches swaying with the wind's ebb and flow. Become a fox cub gambolling across a flower-covered clearing; a badger in its dark cold set.

Role-playing gets you into the moods, qualities, and behaviour of nature's life-forms, grafting them into yourself and allowing you to feel your own heart's and mind's responses to them.

Being a human — Sally the headmistress or John the salesman — sometimes becomes confining. Our enjoyment and appreciation of life depends on our ability to sense the feelings of other creatures, escaping our self-definitions (job title and so on) to taste the joy of self-forgetful empathy with others.

Choose an animal, plant, tree, rock, or mountain — anything — and pretend you *are* that. Coordinate your body and imagination to experience the existence, movements and feelings of that other form of creation. The warm summer breeze flows across your dragonfly wings as you dance among the water reeds. The snow is soft and cold under your fox-paws; your thick fur is protection against the icy wind, but your empty stomach is growling. You hungrily watch a mouse as it scurries across the snow, stopping every few feet to nose in the frozen grasses.

The more you can put your whole being into pretending, the more you'll take on the character and feelings of your subject. The more deeply you can concentrate, the more oneness and sympathetic understanding you'll feel.

Simple scenes like the dandelion parachute or the swaying tree are best for beginners at role-playing. Group practice is good, too — you'll feel less self-conscious when everyone is doing the same thing around you. Try being a snake or a caterpillar inching along; or act out the life-cycle of a beech tree: first the seed in the ground, then the gaining of strength and stature as you become a mighty adult tree, then the rotting and falling, and finally the merging back into the soil from whence you drew your first life. You can act out the whole life cycle in a minute or two. As you gain confidence and concentration you'll have fun with more complicated images.

A flock of mallard (ducks) passes just over the marsh grass, then twists and turns upwards. Each mallard is attuned to the leader, and the flock moves as if it were one bird. You descend gracefully on to the smooth water.

In a different vein: hold a public meeting on whether to build a dam on a certain river. Representatives come

to the meeting — a farmer, a fisherman, a trout, a salmon, a deer, a poplar tree, a water boatman, a kingfisher, a midge, and any others who should be consulted.

Encourage a supporting and non-critical atmosphere when you play this game. Let the child develop at his own pace without fear of comparisons or competition.

SECTION
2

HOW MUCH
I CAN YOU
SEE?

n a new environment children auto-matically set out to prove themselves. They run down steep hills, and try to climb over, under, and through favourite obstacles like fallen trees, cliffs and big rocks. The games in this chapter enlist this kind of adventurous spirit to help make children more sensitively aware of their environment.

Even a simple afternoon walk can be turned into an adventure, with some learning and in-creased awareness included. After we've walked out from our base to our halfway point, I'll fre-quently ask the group if they think they can find the way back. (On the way out I'll have given them help by pointing to landmarks and asking them to look back the way we've come.) There's always a brief period of shock and confusion when they find out it's up to them to lead us back.

After much consultation and some friendly argument, a leader and a direction are chosen. Often I'm accused of giving up the leadership because I don't know the way back myself. But they nearly always find the way back without any help from me . . . even if it takes all night.

We were out on a night hike once, when we heard an owl calling from a distance. We decided to see if we could get close to the owl: but every time we approached, it flew deeper into the forest. Around midnight, when we still hadn't caught up with the owl, we conceded that it was time to go back to base. I asked the boys which was the best route home, and seven fingers pointed to directions spread around a 230-degree arc of the compass!

There was no chance of rain, and it wasn't very cold, so I said they could try to find the way back without my help. The oldest boy took the lead, and I brought up the rear. But it soon became obvious that our leader didn't know the way. His status in the group prevented the others from expressing their doubts; but when we wound back where we'd started, he was quickly deposed and another boy took over the lead. One after another the leaders were chosen, then hopefully exchanged, as we wandered around in the forest night. Finally the boys swallowed their pride and admitted that they couldn't possibly find their way back in the dark.

I sensed that most of them wanted to sleep out and keep trying in the morning. Even though we didn't have sleeping bags or warm coats, we decided to get through the night as best we could, huddling together for warmth. We put the ones who were dressed lightly in the middle, and the rest of us piled on and around them.

This worked fine for about thirty minutes, when the ones who were being crushed on the bottom began squirming their way out of the pile. The boys on the outside then seized their chance for a little warmth and wriggled into the middle. Those on top were cold, and those on the bottom were crushed. Only while temporarily in the middle of the constantly-shifting downward cycle could any of us stay comfortable and warm.

Four hours of squirming later, a dull grey light in the east promised an end to the struggle. We got up and stomped and danced to stay warm while we waited for the sun.

In daylight it was easy for the group to get their bearings and find the way home. We arrived at camp bleary-eyed, but victorious and proud. A year later the same boys begged me for another overnight camp.

You won't necessarily have an experience like this — unless you want to. But the games in this chapter are similar in their ability to make children keenly interested in being as observant of nature as possible.

A.
B. Listening attentively
C. Day and night/ anywhere
D. 1 or more
E. 3 years and up
F. None

Sounds

IN a forest, meadow, marsh, or park, a group of children lie down on their backs with both fists held up in the air. Every time someone hears a new bird song he lifts one finger. Who has the best hearing? This is a wonderful way to make children aware of the sounds (and the stillness) of nature. For fun, see if you can count to ten without hearing a bird song. Vary

the game by listening for general animal sounds — or for any sounds at all, like wind in the grass, falling leaves, rushing water.

To get children to concentrate more deeply on any natural setting, ask them how many different colours and shades of colours they can see in front of them without moving from where they are standing.

A.
B. Observation
C. Day/anywhere
D. 1 or more
E. 4 years and up
F. None

Colours

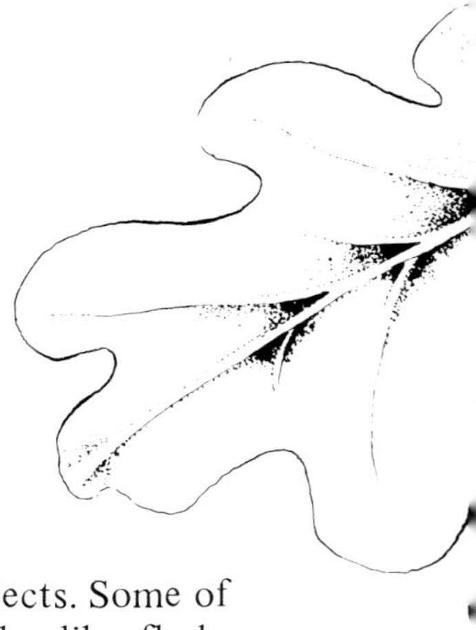

THIS GAME is played
primarily to introduce
the concepts of camouflage
(protective colouring) and
adaptation.

Choose a 40- to 50-foot
section of footpath and place
along it 10 to 15 man-made objects. Some of
them should stand out brightly, like flash-
bulbs or balloons. Others should blend with
their surroundings, and therefore be more difficult to pick
out. Keep the number of objects you've planted secret.

The children walk over the section of trail one at a
time, with intervals between them, trying to spot (but
not pick up) as many of the objects as they can. When
they reach the end of the trail, they whisper in your ear
how many they saw. If no one saw all of them, tell everyone how many were seen, but that "There are still more!"
Then let them start again.

End the game with a discussion of the ways colour
camouflage helps animals. Then go on a search for small
camouflaged animals (insects, spiders, etc.).

Unnature Trail

A.
B. Camouflage, observation
C. Day/forest, thicket
D. 1-12
E. 5-13 years
F. Man-made litter

A.
B. Concentration, developing the senses
C. Day/forest, thicket
D. 2 - 7 (per leader)
E. 6 years and up
F. Blindfolds

TAKE your children to a secluded, secret spot. After blindfolding them, arrange them in a line, caterpillar-fashion, with each child placing their hands on the shoulders of the child ahead. Tell them that as you lead them along they are to listen to, smell, and feel their surroundings as completely as they can. Make frequent stops along the way at points of interest, such as unusual trees and rocks, or to smell a fragrant flower or bush. The more variety there is along the route, the better. To add variety, walk on and off paths, walk through clumps of bracken, or go in and out of sunny forest clearings.

When you have gone as far as you think is appropriate, remove the blindfolds. The children must now try to find their way back along the route to the starting point. Sometimes, before they turn back I'll ask them to draw a picture or map of what they think the course and the areas we passed through look like. This helps them to translate into pictures the sounds, smells and touches they've experienced. The sound of ducks might indicate a pond or marsh; fragrance would mean flowers. As much as possible, allow the children to find the way back on their own.

Caution: blind caterpillars more than six segments long quickly become entangled and hard to manage.

Caterpillar Walk

A.
B. Exploring,
   developing the
   senses
C. Day/anywhere
D. 2 or more
E. 6 years and up
F. Blindfolds

THIS is a shorter version of Caterpillar Walk. Blindfold your child (or children) and tell him you are going to lead him to a spot not too far away. Ask him to explore his surroundings with his hands until he knows the spot well. When he is satisfied, lead him back — still blindfolded — to the starting point. Take the blindfold off and ask him to find the spot he explored with his hands.

& Back Home

THIS is a good game for getting children interested in rocks, plants, and animals. Before assembling the children to play, secretly gather from the immediate area about 10 common natural objects, such as stones, seeds, pine cones, plant parts, and some signs of animal activity. Lay the objects out on a handkerchief and cover them with another handkerchief. Collect the children around you and tell them, *"Under this cloth are 10 natural objects that you'll be able to find nearby. I will lift the handkerchief for 25 seconds so you can take a good look and try to remember everything you see."*

After looking at the objects, the children spread out and collect identical items, keeping their findings to themselves. After five minutes of searching, call them back, dramatically pull out the objects from under the handkerchief, one at a time, telling interesting stories about each one. As each object is presented, ask the children if they found one just like it.

Children have a lively curiosity about the kinds of things you'll show them — rocks, seeds, plants, and so on. When you repeat the game several times, it has a noticeable strengthening effect on the child's concentration and memory.

Duplication

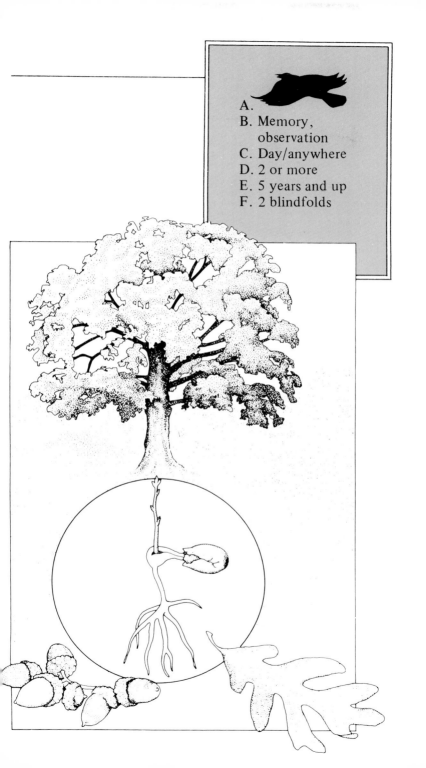

A.
B. Memory, observation
C. Day/anywhere
D. 2 or more
E. 5 years and up
F. 2 blindfolds

A.

B. Observation of soil surface
C. Day/anywhere
D. 1 or more
E. 4 years and up
F. 3 to 5 ft strings, magnifying glasses

Micro-Hike

A MICRO-HIKE is a very short expedition guided by a string three to five feet long. The "hikers" cover the trail inch by inch on their bellies, viewing such natural wonders as grass blades bent by rainbow dewdrops, colourful beetles sprinkled with flower pollen, and powerful-jawed eight-eyed spiders. Because young children are particularly fond of tiny objects, their intense absorption in the world of the forest-in-miniature will amaze you.

Begin by asking the children to span their strings over the most interesting ground they can find. Give each

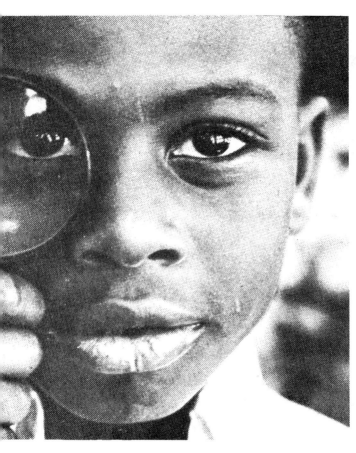

child a magical magnifying glass, to shrink himself down to the size of an ant. Tell the children that they must keep their eyes no higher than one foot above the ground.

You may want to ask them questions to stimulate their imaginations: *"What kind of world are you travelling through right now? Who are your nearest neighbours? Are they friendly? Do they work hard? What is that spider going to do – eat you, or take you for a ride? What would it be like to be that metallic green beetle? How does he spend his day?"*

SECTION
3

NATURE'S
NBALANCE

Nowadays, children get lots of instruction in the textbook concepts of ecology. By contrast, the main emphasis in this book is on developing their inner and intuitive qualities. Yet feelings alone sometimes aren't enough, especially when those feelings aren't shared by others. Years ago I had an experience that first made me aware of this truth. It also caused me to want to balance my intuitive understanding of nature with a stronger scientific background.

At the back of the farm where I lived there was a small brush-covered slough (a piece of low, muddy, swampy land). I spent most of my free hours there, and another creature came there often, too — a hawk. I'd find her roosting on one of the dead oaks, where she liked to *perch for the unobstructed view of the surrounding area. After several months she became so used to me that she'd stay on her perch even when I walked close to her.*

During the day I was in the habit of climbing to the farmhouse roof to look out over the orchards at the surrounding country. From there I could also see if the hawk was at her post, 150 yards away. As the months passed, a feeling of friendship developed between us.

One morning just after I'd returned from a few days' absence, I walked out to the slough to see if everything was okay. To my shock, I found that all of the oaks were felled and burning, and that a man was just about to fell the last tree — the hawk's favourite.

I tried to persuade him to leave the tree standing, but he said it wasn't doing any good so he might as well cut it down and burn it. I said there wasn't any possibility of it falling on his orchard, and because it was dead it wasn't using up any water or soil nutrients. But he wouldn't be moved, and the tree was on his land, so there wasn't much else I could do. After the oaks were cut down I rarely saw the hawk again.

My heart had spoken out to the tree-cutter, but I didn't have the facts to support my feelings. I felt there must be <u>some</u> important reasons why dead trees are valuable; but at the time I didn't <u>know</u> any of those reasons. Later, I did find information that might have helped the man understand the possible negative consequences of chopping down those oaks. For instance, dead trees provide homes for many birds — like woodpeckers and nuthatches — that rid the land of harmful insect pests.

THIS GAME requires at least six players. Give each child a slip of paper and have him secretly write on it the name of a plant or animal that lives in the area. The players are going to build a pyramid, just as they might do in gym class; but don't tell them this until after you've collected all the slips of paper. Now the fun begins: *"From what source does the earth get its energy? ... From the sun! ... Right. What form of life is the first to make use of that energy? ... Plants! ... Right again. Now we're going to build a pyramid."*

A few groans may be heard when the "plant children" realize their fate.

"The plants will be on the bottom, because all ani-

*mals depend on them direct-
ly or indirectly for food. All
the plants kneel down here
on all fours, close together
in a line. Now, as I read off
the animals from the slips of
paper, tell me whether they
are plant-eaters or meat-
eaters. All the plant-eaters
(herbivores) stand in a line
behind the plants. All the meat-eaters (carnivores) stand
in another line behind the herbivores."*

A.
B. Balance of nature, food chain
C. Day/clearing
D. 6 or more
E. 7 years and up
F. Pencils and paper

There will nearly always be more children in the
upper-level groups than in the supporting plant levels;
it's a lot more fun to be a deer or beaver than
it is to be a dandelion or a shrew. Humility, alas,
seldom stimulates the imagination. With so many tops
and so few bottoms, it will be impossible to build a
stable pyramid. Some of the predators will just have
to forfeit their exalted status. Challenge the children
to reconstruct their own pyramid into one that will
easily support all its members. (Tell them the bigger
children can change to plants if they wish.) Clearly,
the higher up in the food chain, the fewer animals there
are. Demonstrate the importance of plants by pretending
to pull one of them out of the pyramid.

Pyramid of Life

$\mathbf{G}$IVE each child an imaginary deed to one square mile of land. On this virgin plot he will be free to create his own dream-forest, complete with as many trees, animals, mountains and rivers as he desires. Let their imaginations run wild. To encourage creativity you can give the children some suggestions:

"*To make your forest beautiful and radiant, you might want to add things like waterfalls and windstorms,*

Recipe for

A.
B. Appreciating nature, ecology
C. Day/forest
D. 2 or more
E. 7 years and up
F. Pencils and index cards

or perpetual rainbows . . . "

Ask them to list the ingredients of their forest, then let them draw a picture of it. End by discussing with them whether their individual forests are able to maintain themselves year after year. For instance, see if they have chosen representatives of the food cycle: plant-eaters, plants, and decomposers (example: ants, mushrooms, bacteria). Don't let them forget subtle factors like soil and climate.

a Forest

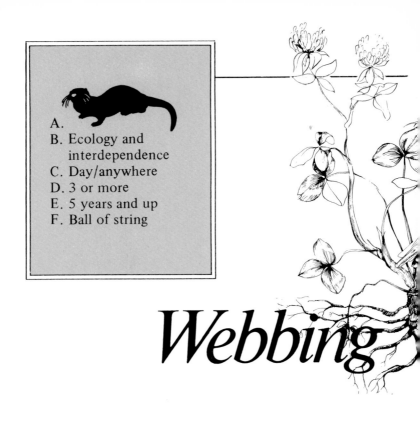

A.
B. Ecology and
   interdependence
C. Day/anywhere
D. 3 or more
E. 5 years and up
F. Ball of string

Webbing

HERE IS A GAME that makes very clear the essential interrelationships among all the members of nature's community. Webbing vividly portrays how air, rocks, plants, and animals function together in a balanced web of life.

The children form a circle. The leader stands inside the circle near the edge, with a ball of string: *"Who can name a plant that grows in this area? . . . dandelion . . . Good. Here, Miss Dandelion, you hold the end of the string. Is there an animal living around here that might eat the dandelion? . . . Rabbits! . . . Ah, a sumptuous meal. Mr. Rabbit, you take hold of the string here, you are connected to Miss Dandelion by your dependence on her flowers for your lunch. Now, who needs Mr. Rabbit for his lunch?"*

Continue connecting the children with string as their relationships to the rest of the group emerge. Bring in new elements and considerations, such as other animals, soil, water and so on, until the entire circle of children is strung together in a symbol of the web of life. You have created your own ecosystem.

To demonstrate how each individual is important to the whole community, take away by some plausible means one member of the web. For example, a fire or a farmer kills a tree. When the tree falls, it tugs on the strings it holds; anyone who feels a tug in his string is in some way affected by the death of the tree. Now everyone who felt a tug from the tree gives a tug. The process continues until every individual is shown to be affected by the destruction of the tree.

Predator-

A.
B. Imitating animal
behaviour
C. Day/clearing
D. 6 or more
E. 5 years and up
F. Bells, blindfolds

THIS GAME introduces food chains and the way they work in nature. In an open clearing, form a circle about 15 feet across. Blindfold two of the children and get them to stand in the circle. Ask one of the children to name a predator that lives in the area, and ask the other child to name a prey. The predator tries to catch his prey by listening for him, then tracking him down and catching him. If either animal goes too near the edge of the circle, the children tap him twice. Stress the need for silence while the game is in progress, and have the players make things more realistic by imitating the animals they've chosen to be. For variety, experiment with different numbers of predators and prey. Put bells on some of the animals, forcing them to modify their strategy of hunting or of avoiding capture. If your predator is not as bold as he could be, and interest is lagging, tighten up the circle, bringing the predator and his prey closer together.

Prey

A.
B. Careful observation, plant succession
C. Day/pond edge
D. 1 or more
E. 10 years and up
F. Pencils and paper

Plant Succession Crawl

PLANT succession is the process by which soil and water conditions of an area gradually change, allowing new species to come in and eventually establish themselves, and forcing old species to migrate to more favourable conditions. A very good place for observing plant succession is the area just around a pond, especially if there is a gentle slope running up away from the water. As you move further away from the centre, the soil becomes drier and its composition changes. You will be able to observe several plant types in successive rings around the pond. To see the actual process of plant succession, you would have to watch the changes in and around a pond over a period of many years. This is because plant succession is the result of plants dying and slowly building up and drying out the soil. When the soil becomes drier, the plants that like wet soil are easily forced out by their dry-soil competitors. Over a long period a pond will actually shrink and disappear as the soil level builds

up higher and
higher around it. The rings
of plant life move gradually
closer to the centre of the pond
as the wet area becomes smaller.
You can see this process of plant mi-
gration happening by careful observation
at any one of its points; it is rather like
looking at one frame of a cine film.
Ask the children to crawl from the outside
rings toward the edge of the water. By crawling and closely examining the ground, they
will get a feeling for the different soil conditions
needed by the different types of plants in the
rings. Ask the children to share their discoveries
as they find them. One discovery might be
coming across a new ring with its special kinds
of trees, shrubs, plants and grasses, or wetter
and stronger-smelling soil. When he reaches
the water, tell each child to draw a map
of the pond and its surrounding area, with
the successive circles of plant life. Label
each ring from wettest to driest, and
list the plants that grow there.
Ask the children to imagine how
big the pond will be in fifty
or a hundred
years.

SECTION
4

LEARNING
I IS FUN

_try my best to make learning fun
and exciting for children. One way I do this is to
point out characteristics that animals and plants
have in common with man. Before taking children to a pond, for instance, I'll talk with them
for a while about aquatic insects:_

_"What things do humans use to help them
move and breathe in water?"_

_"Flippers. Wet suits. Oxygen tanks. Oars. Nets.
Diving masks."_

_"Did you know that aquatic insects have the
same needs, and use the same equipment, as man
does? For example, there are diving beetles that
use scuba tanks: they trap a silvery bubble of air
under a thick layer of hair, then use it to breathe
underwater. Some diving beetles even carry an
air-bubble 'tank' along behind them. A beetle's
breathing system is more efficient than our scuba
tanks, though, because beetles don't need com-_

pressed air, and they can fill their tanks with oxygen from the surrounding water. With his diving tank, a beetle can stay underwater for as long as thirty-six hours! Diving beetles also have waxy hairs that make them float — just like a wet suit. If they aren't swimming or holding on to something, they bob right up to the surface.

"Most aquatic insects use the breast stroke when they swim, although a few prefer the crawl. But there is one insect who likes the backstroke so much that he's been named the 'back swimmer'. He is shaped like a boat, with a keel running down his back and two long, oar-like legs at his sides.

"Then there is the black fly larva, who lives in the fast rapids of a stream. He moves along carefully while fastened to a safety rope. If the stream carries him away, he can crawl back along the rope to his original position. The black fly larva often reaches adult size while still underwater. To keep his wings from getting wet he rides up out of the water inside a bubble of air — like a submarine!"

Children are captivated by bizarre tales of these underwater creatures. They're always excited by the chance to comb through aquatic vegetation for bugs with kitchen strainers. Once the search begins, I find myself bounding from one shriek of delight to another as they call to me to come and see their findings.

A class of eleven year-olds had just finished hunting for insects, when a water truck drove up to the tiny pond and lowered its hose into the water. When the driver started his pump, the children immediately realized that the insects would later be spread out on the road, and die. So several of them went up to the driver and pleaded with him to put a fine screen over the hose. The man was friendly; touched by the children's concern, he said he would be happy to install the screen. Afterwards the children introduced him to their aquatic friends.

It's fascinating to discover how different life forms live. The games in this chapter create an atmosphere of excitement that stimulates the child's curiosity and concentration.

A.
B. Animal classification, animal ecology
C. Day/clearing or road
D. 4 or more
E. 7 years and up
F. None

THE ANIMAL GAME is an entertaining way to review zoology and animal ecology. Dramatic climaxes surprise the players again and again, and make for lots of excitement and laughter.

Form two equal teams. Each team chooses an animal and then thinks up six to eight riddle clues for that animal. The clues should be progressively easier, proceeding from the general to the specific. You'll find a list of sample clues below.

When both teams have their clues ready, ask them to face each other across a line made with sticks or drawn in the sand. Fifteen feet behind each team draw another line, which will be that team's base. (See diagram on the next page.)

The teams take turns giving clues. (Each team decides beforehand which members will give which clues.) Team A gives its first clue, then team B tries to guess the identity of team A's animal. If the guess is wrong, nothing happens. Now team B gives its first clue, and team A tries to guess team B's animal, but they also guess wrong, so still nothing happens. As the clues become more and more obvious, the tension mounts. This continues until one of the teams guesses correctly. For example, team A says. "I don't lay my eggs in my own nest," and team B guesses, "Are you a cuckoo?"

Animal Game

The members of team A turn nervously towards their base, while team B hovers eagerly over them. One of team A's members says, "Yes!" and team A streaks for its base with team B in hot pursuit.

Here are some sample clues that will give you an idea of the thought processes a child goes through in playing this game. Take a piece of paper and cover all the clues except the first. After you read the clue, try to guess the answer. Continue down the page until you've gone through all the clues. Check your final guess against the coded answer. To decipher the code, write down the letters that follow alphabetically the letters in the code. You'll find ten more sets of clues on page 132.

Example: C N F = D O G

1. I have four feet, and my body temperature stays the same.
2. I do not hibernate.
3. My habitat is the forest, especially pine forest.
4. My front teeth are constantly growing, so I gnaw a lot.
5. My diet includes pine cones, nuts, seeds, buds, insects and fungi.
6. Owls, golden eagles and stoats are some of the animals that eat me.
7. My tail is nearly as long as my body.
8. I change my coat twice a year. In winter I'm dull and grey, but I'm named after my handsome chestnut red summer coat.

Q D C   R P T H Q Q D K

TEAM A's BASE

TEAMS $\frac{A\ A\ A\ A\ A\ A\ A}{B\ B\ B\ B\ B\ B\ B}$

TEAM B's BASE

A.
B. Animal classification, animal ecology
C. Day/anywhere
D. 2 or more
E. 6 years and up
F. Animal pictures, safety pins

What Animal Am I?

PIN A PICTURE of an animal on the back of one of the children in the group. Don't show him the picture. Have him turn around so that all the other children can see what animal he has become. He then asks questions to discover his own identity. The other children can answer only yes, no, and maybe.

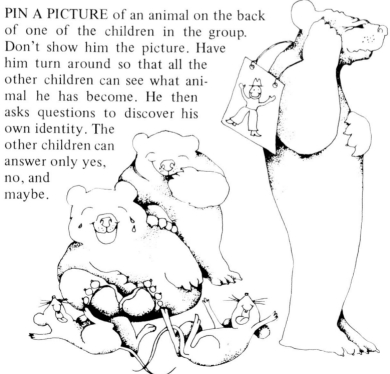

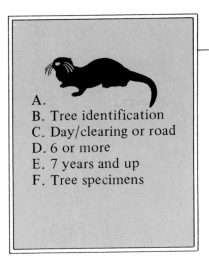

A.
B. Tree identification
C. Day/clearing or road
D. 6 or more
E. 7 years and up
F. Tree specimens

THIS GAME is a lot like Steal the Bacon, but it has been adapted to help children identify and remember the trees and shrubs in an area. As you explore the locality where you'll be playing the game, collect small samples of leaves, flowers, and seeds from the trees and bushes — you'll need about 7-10 specimens in all.

Form two equal teams and line them up facing each other, 30 feet apart. Put the plant specimens in a row on the ground between the two teams. The teams count off separately, so that each player has a number, and in each team there are players numbered one, two, three, etc.

When the teams are ready, call out the name of a tree or bush represented by one of the specimens lying between the teams, then call out a number. (To add surprise, call the numbers out of sequence.)

"The next plant is a beech tree, and the number is . . . three!"

As soon as the "threes" hear their number called, they race to the specimens, trying to be first to find the beech twig. Every successful player earns two points for his team. Picking up the wrong specimen results in a loss of two points.

Identification Game

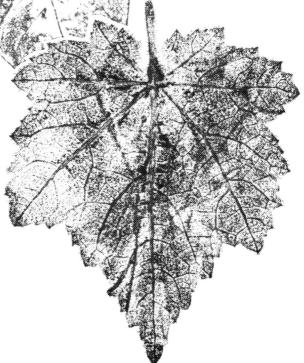

A.
B. Revision of facts and concepts
C. Day/clearing or road
D. 6 or more
E. 5 - 13 years
F. None

THIS is an excellent game for reviewing newly-learned concepts. Divide the group into two equal teams, the Owls and the Crows. Line up the two teams facing each other, about two feet apart. About 15 feet behind each team, draw another line for Base. The leader makes a statement aloud, and if the statement is true the Owls chase the Crows, trying to catch them before they reach their own Base. If the statement is false, the Crows chase the Owls. Anyone caught must join the other team.

If the answer isn't obvious to the players, you'll get

Owls & Crows

some of the Owls and Crows running towards each other, and others running back to their Bases. During the pandemonium, the leader should remain silent and neutral. When the action has calmed down, he can reveal the correct answer.

Here are some sample statements: Sensory: *"The wind is coming from behind the Crows."* Conceptual: *"A deciduous tree keeps its leaves all year long."* Observational: (after showing them a leaf) *"The leaf had five points and five veins."* Identification: *"This seed comes from an oak tree."*

FIND A PLACE WHERE several different kinds of trees are growing. One child shapes his body to look like a particular species and the other children try to guess what kind of tree he is. A group can also play this game by dividing up into teams: a whole team can portray a tree, or the group can choose a member who most resembles the species they want to represent.

You can vary the game by impersonating animals, or you can leave it open, with the condition that the object must be something in nature — no sports cars or dump trucks, please! This game helps the members of a group feel comfortable with each other, and also develops dramatic skills.

A.
B. Imitation,
   tree shapes
C. Day/forest
D. 2 or more
E. 5 years and up
F. None

Tree
Silhouettes

A.
B. Identification, observation
C. Day/anywhere
D. 3 or more
E. 5 - 14 years
F. Paper bags, pencils, scavenger lists

Scavenger Hunt

SCAVENGER HUNTS are probable familiar to you from your own childhood. This one is adapted to finding natural objects. You should assign scavenger lists that require the child to think creatively or to look very closely. I've suggested some ideas (see opposite), but you will need to prepare your own list from things the children can find locally.

*17. Everything in nature has a function. *21.Every thing in nature is important (even poisonous berries are important to the birds that eat them). *24. A sun trap is anything that captures the sun's heat (water, rocks, plants, animals).

Scavenger List

Collect only things that you can
return safely and without damage.

1. A feather
2. One seed dispersed by the wind
3. Exactly 100 of something
4. A beech leaf
5. A thorn
6. A bone
7. Three different kinds of seeds
8. One camouflaged animal or insect
9. Something round
10. Part of an egg
11. Something fuzzy
12. Something sharp
13. A piece of fur
14. Five pieces of man-made litter
15. Something perfectly straight
16. Something beautiful
17. Something that is of no use in nature*
18. A chewed leaf, (not by you!)
19. Something that makes a noise
20. Something white
21. Something important in nature*
22. Something that reminds you of yourself
23. Something soft
24. A sun trap*
25. A big smile

Wild Animal Scramble

CHILDREN show keen interest in animal classification — normally not a terribly exciting subject — when you introduce it through the Wild Animal Scramble.

Write the names of common animals on index cards. (Pictures are even better, if available, because they stimulate more interest and enable the players to give more accurate responses.) Pin one animal card or picture on the back of each player. At your signal, the players take turns asking questions to get clues to their own identities. Encourage them to question everyone in the group. The players can ask as many questions as they want, but answers are limited to yes, no, and maybe. (Sometimes, before starting, I've found it necessary to discuss with them the kinds of questions that will help to narrow down the possibilities.)

As soon as each player feels certain that he knows the name of his animal, let him write down his name and what he thinks he is. After everyone has finished, begin the "award ceremony". Call the players one at a time up on to a rock, stump or log, with their backs to the rest of the group. Then announce what the player's guess was. Encourage the audience to applaud correct guesses. Besides teaching the concept of animal classification, this game also helps bring out three important qualities:

1. Open-mindedness: avoiding preconceptions and snap judgments. *"Let's see, I live in the forest; I'm warm-blooded; I'm active at night, and I have four legs. Well, that means I'm a badger."* (Actually, the correct answer might have been *"a fox."*)

A.
B. Animal classification, animal ecology
C. Day and night/ anywhere
D. 4 or more
E. 7 years and up
F. Index cards, straight pins

2. Discrimination: using new information, and testing the validity of new information. Sometimes players are mistakenly given false answers to their questions. *(a) "I can swim, and I'm warm-blooded. (Then I have to be a bird or a mammal. What birds and mammals swim?)" (b) "A member of the rodent family? But I'm a predator. I think I can discount Jerry's answer, because no rodents are predators. Besides, I have dog-like tracks. I bet I'm a fox. I'll ask Adam if I have a high-pitched howl."*

3. Concern for others: one of the features I like best about this game is the concern and encouragement the players show towards each other. Many players feel they haven't really finished the game until everyone else has guessed his animal correctly. Often I've seen six or seven players gathered around the last one, encouraging him on to the end.

An Optional Variation. Listed below are starter questions that will help you narrow down the choice to a few animal groups (i.e., mammals, insects, mollusks, etc.). If you want to know more about the characteristics of individual animal groups, I recommend that you read a biology textbook, or buy *The Young Naturalist's Handbook* by Leonard Moore, published by Hamlyn, which is an illustrated guide to the wildlife of Britain and Europe.

1. *"Am I a vertebrate (animal with a backbone)?"*

If the answer is yes, there are five possibilities: fish,

amphibians, reptiles, birds, mammals.

To divide the vertebrates into still smaller groups, ask if the animal is cold- or warm-blooded. "Cold-blooded vertebrate" means the animal's body temperature changes to match changes in the temperature of the surrounding environment. Cold-blooded vertebrates are fish, amphibians and reptiles.

"Warm-blooded vertebrate" means the animal maintains the same body temperature, regardless of whether it is cold or hot outside. The warm-blooded vertebrates are birds and mammals.

2. If the answer is no (not a vertebrate animal), it means the animal is an *in*vertebrate (animal with no backbone). Here is a list of the more common invertebrates: *Annelids* (worms, leeches), *Echinoderms* (starfish), *Mollusks* (snails, clams), *Crustaceans* (crabs, crayfish), *Centipedes, Millipedes, Spiders, Insects.*

To divide the invertebrates into smaller categories, ask *"Do I have jointed legs?"* (Invertebrates with jointed legs are: *crustaceans, centipedes, millipedes, spiders, insects.* Invertebrates without jointed legs are: *annelids, echinoderms, mollusks.)*

Listed here are some questions that will help you narrow your choices even further: *Am I a predator? . . . Can I swim . . . Can I fly? . . . Do I live in the (ocean, desert, etc.)? . . . Do I have (2, 4, 6, 8, or more than 8) legs? (You can only ask one question at a time!) . . . Am I brightly coloured? . . . Am I active at night?*

How come Noah only caught two fish ???

A.
B. Animal movement and behaviour
C. Day and hight/ anywhere
D. 6 or more
E. 5 years and up
F. Index cards, pencil

THE IDEA is to find your mate amid the herd of cavorting beasts and birds on Noah's Ark. Begin by counting the number of players in your group, then make a list of animals half as long as the list of players.

Write the name of each animal on two cards. When you finish there should be as many cards in your hand as there are players in the group — one card for each player. If you have an odd number of players, write the name of one of the animals on three cards, making a threesome to accommodate the extra player.

Shuffle the cards and pass them out. Each child reads his card and becomes the animal whose name is on the card, keeping his identity a secret. Now collect the cards again.

On signal, the players all begin acting out the sounds, shapes, and typical movements of their animals, with the intention of attracting their mates. The action is hilarious when all the animals begin baying, croaking, screeching, whistling, strutting, flapping, leaping, and posing. They can make all the noise they want, but talking is prohibited — each animal must attract his mate solely by the authenticity of his behaviour. The game ends in happy reunions and much laughter.

Noah's Ark

'Cause he only had two worms.

A.
B. Animal characteris-
   tics, movement, and
   behaviour
C. Day and night/
   anywhere
D. 3-6 in a group
E. 7 years and up
F. None

THIS GAME is for groups of four or five children. Ask each group to select an animal common to the area. Then tell them that each group will have to imitate the body of their animal. They are going to appear before an "animal expert" or "panel of experts" who will try to guess their identity on the basis of the movements and behaviour they act out. No noise is allowed, except what they can make with props (optional) such as a tin can with pebbles in it to mimic the rattle of a rattlesnake.

Give the groups about five minutes to work on their acts: *"Oh, no! A scorpion has eight legs – we'll all have to be legs! . . . I can be the head, too, since I'm up front and my arms can be the pincers. . . . Okay, I'll be the tail, but I don't think I can hold it too long. You guys will have to bend forward and hold onto each other to make the body. Ready?"*

Animal Parts

SECTION
5

PLAY AND
T DISCOVERY

he games shared here are filled
with hilarity, suspense and adventure, and are indeed great fun. I believe that nature games are a
fine stepping stone to lead the child into a deeper appreciation of the natural world. My greatest
concern is that children have joyous first experiences with the natural world. This way, their
associations with the natural world begin on a
happy note, and will always be fond ones.

In spirit, these games are like those which
Indian boys used to play: stalking animals
and "enemies"; moving soundlessly; learning to
be unseen even by wary eyes; training ears to
catch and recognize every sound, eyes to miss
not a single detail; and practising quickness of
foot and agility of movement. The games of the

Indian boy became the survival skills of the hunter, providing food and bringing him into intimate communion with the land on which he lived and the creatures among whom he walked.

Catch the Horse

AT one nature camp where I worked there was an eight-acre area of tall grass. We used to section off a small portion for games involving exploring, hiding, and running. On that magnificent little piece of grassland we played Catch the Horse in grand fashion.

"In the old days," we told the children, *"the villagers would often lose their horses in the fields, and so someone would have to climb a tree to try and spot them. The person in the tree would wave directions to those chasing the horse."* At the centre we stationed a child in a tree, with a big red flag for signalling. The horse took his head start, then the search began. The horse would be spotted many times, but would usually escape before the searchers could close in. The lookout would then give new directions, and the children would once more go off in hot pursuit.

The children enjoyed playing in the field so much that they reacted with indignation whenever we told them that it would have to be burned. (The centre set fire to the grass every two years to prevent it from turning into a forest.) Again and again, I've seen that if people have a positive, joyful first encounter with some aspect of nature, they will become protective

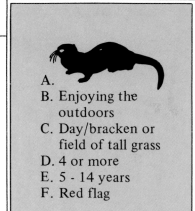

A.
B. Enjoying the outdoors
C. Day/bracken or field of tall grass
D. 4 or more
E. 5 - 14 years
F. Red flag

toward that life form or environment.

Wheatfields, tall-grass and bracken are ideal sites for this game. Choose from the group the one member (possibly an adult) who has the best agility and endurance — he will be the "horse". While everyone else closes their eyes, the horse takes a three-minute head start. When time is up, everyone begins hunting through the brush to try and flush out the horse. Whoever spots him first calls to the others to join the chase.

I especially remember playing horse for a group of 8 year-olds, dodging their charges and lunges for a good fifteen or twenty minutes. Several times their teacher organized them for circling manoeuvres, but each time I was just barely able to slip through the closing net. In the end we were all completely exhausted from crashing through the undergrowth. The momentum of countless circles I'd run around the children flung me dizzily to the earth, and as I turned over on my back the children piled on top of me. Their diving forms, the grass and the trees, the liquid sky all appeared to revolve overhead in vast, sweeping circles. We lay there totally spent, but savouring an awesome state of oneness with the land.

A.
B. Calmness,
   observation
C. Night/road or trail
D. 4 or more
E. 7 years and up
F. Torches

Camouflage

A GOOD TIME to play Camouflage is on the way home from a night hike; but you can also play it on those wonderful summer evenings when dusk is just turning to nightfall. Divide the group into two teams, hiders and searchers. The hiders scatter along a designated section of the path. How close to the path they will hide depends on the brightness of the moon and whether or not the searchers have torches. Since each hider's whole body must be in full view from at least one point along the path, they will have to try to blend with the profiles of natural objects around them to remain unseen.

The American Indian hunter, who sometimes donned camouflage costume for the purpose, also tried to think like and enter into the conscious of the animal or object he was impersonating. He knew that the deer, bear, or bird he hunted could detect his presence not just with its eyes, nose, and ears, but with an ability to "sense" a man's presence. The hiders can try to tune in to this intuitive faculty, which we humans also have, by trying to feel that they are a natural part of the objects around them; and the searchers can try to sense a foreign presence among the rocks and leaves. As soon as all the searchers pass by him (they should travel close together), each hider can reveal himself.

A.
B. Excitement, intense alertness, stalking
C. Day/bracken thicket, forest
D. 13 or more
E. 9 years and up
F. Beans, noisemakers

BRAVE young adventurers make their way to safety through a forest and bracken infested with wildmen.

Find a bushy, tangly area seamed with paths, or any terrain with good cover. A thick wood is ideal (if free of nightshade or poison ivy!). You will need to mark out the boundaries of your "wildman woods". The size of the area depends on how many people are playing and how good the cover is. If the terrain is bracken, or fairly open woodland, or if you have a large group, you'll want to broaden the boundaries.

Pick five to eight adults or older children to act as wildmen. They should dress to fit their ferocious roles, applying mud and tomato sauce for gory effect and equipping themselves with a variety of noisemakers. The wildmen scatter through the thicket ready to catch — or at least liven things up for — anyone they meet.

Wildmen in the Alders

Before entering the woods, each child is given four beans. Each time he is caught, the wildman demands one of his beans. He must duly hand over the bean and return to the starting line to try again. If he loses all his beans, it is all right to give him more. Players returning to the start should go around the outside of the playing area, to avoid confusing the wildmen.

How much fun the children have depends largely on the attitude of the wildmen. Instead of collecting as many beans as they can, the wildmen should try to give the other children a good time: providing close escapes by coming within an inch of catching someone, then tripping on a root with a loud cry of dismay. The wildmen can set traps for the faster children, while somehow letting the slower ones slip by. Children love a good scare and will talk about it for days afterwards.

When the children are assembled and ready, call out to the wildmen to *"make some noise and let us know if you're in there"*. The ensuing din of bird calls, whistles, bangings, tin pans and screechings, orchestrated into one grand horrible noise, will add greatly to the excitement of entering the forest.

Sleeping Miser

A.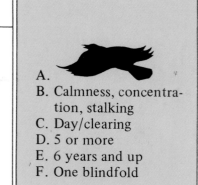
B. Calmness, concentration, stalking
C. Day/clearing
D. 5 or more
E. 6 years and up
F. One blindfold

CHOOSE one person in your group to be Sleeping Miser. The rest of the group will be stalkers. The miser sits blindfolded on the ground, jealously guarding an object of great value that rests in front of him. (You can use a rock or a flag.) But a miser can't stay awake forever guarding his treasure, and he has fallen asleep.

The stalkers form a ring around the miser, about 30 paces away (you can reduce the distance if there is noisy ground cover). At a signal, the stalkers begin to advance as quietly as possible (encourage them to go barefoot if they wish). They must try to get close enough to steal the treasure without waking up the miser; so they will need to be aware and in control of every movement of their bodies. If the miser clearly hears an approaching stalker, he points in that direction. If his finger points true or nearly true, the stalker must freeze. There is usually some debate, so a referee is helpful.

When a number of stalkers have been frozen, stop the game and allow the frozen ones to go back to the perimeter and start again. This way, no one will be left out of the game for very long. Make sure no one advances during this break. On signal, everyone again begins sneaking up on the miser. Allow no running or diving for the treasure. The stalker who succeeds in capturing the treasure is Miser for the next game.

Because everyone is very quiet during Sleeping Miser, there is a good chance of seeing the more secretive animals if you are out in a wild place. This is also a good game for calming down a too-rumbustious group of children.

A.
B. Enjoying the out-
   doors, concentration
C. Day/clearing or road
D. 6 or more
E. 5 years and up
F. One blindfold

Bat & Moth

LET all the group form a circle 10 to 15 feet across. Choose a member of the circle to be the bat, then ask him to come to the centre of the circle to be blindfolded. Designate three to five other children as moths and ask them also to come to the centre of the circle. The bat tries to catch the moths.

Whenever the bat calls out *"Bat!"* the moths call back *"Moth!"* Tell the moths: *"Every time you hear the bat call out 'Bat!' it's his radar signal hitting you. He sends it out to see if there's anything out there. His cry bounces off you and returns to him like a radar signal. The return signal is the word 'Moth!' that you shout. Now he knows moths are near – and he's ready to eat!"*

The bat tracks down and tags the moths by listening to their responses. It takes good concentration to be a successful bat. So this game is good for developing concentration, especially when the bat must chase several moths at the same time.

Add some excitement by bringing two bats into the circle at once. Encourage the bats to hunt as a team. I usually choose a tall bat and a short one, so they won't bang heads if they bump into each other.

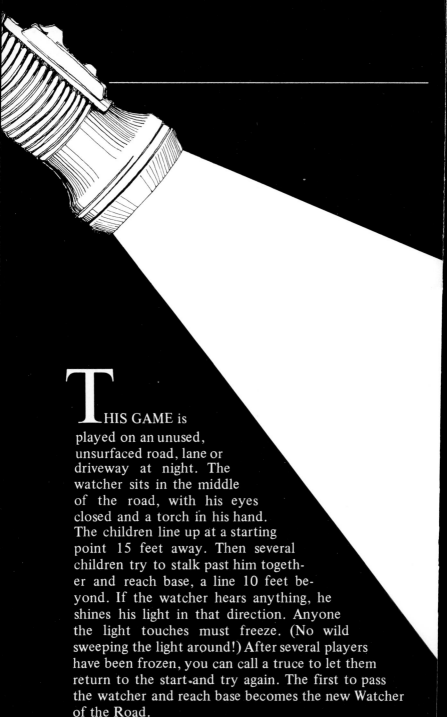

THIS GAME is
played on an unused,
unsurfaced road, lane or
driveway at night. The
watcher sits in the middle
of the road, with his eyes
closed and a torch in his hand.
The children line up at a starting
point 15 feet away. Then several
children try to stalk past him together and reach base, a line 10 feet be-
yond. If the watcher hears anything, he
shines his light in that direction. Anyone
the light touches must freeze. (No wild
sweeping the light around!) After several players
have been frozen, you can call a truce to let them
return to the start and try again. The first to pass
the watcher and reach base becomes the new Watcher
of the Road.

A.
B. Calmness, concen-
   tration, stalking
C. Night/road
D. 5 or more
E. 5 - 13 years
F. Torch

Watcher
of the
Road

SPOTTING AND ATTRACTING ANIMALS

Almost everyone loves to watch animals. I feel this is because animals seem to us to have a certain quality of innocence and spontaneity; they are a constant reminder that all creatures — including ourselves — have a right to a free and contented life.

I remember an experience I had as a boy that awakened in me a life-long fascination for marshes, and for a life lived wild and free. I was playing alone out of doors on a cold, foggy morning when suddenly I heard a startling chorus of "whouks" coming towards me through the air. I peered intently at the thick fog, hoping for at least a glimpse of the geese. Seconds passed; the tempo of their cries increased. They were going to fly directly overhead! I could hear their wings slapping only yards above me. All of a sudden, bursting through a gap in the fog, came a large

SECTION
6

flock of pearl-white snow geese. I was as if the sky had given birth to them. For five or six wonderful seconds their sleek and graceful forms were visible, then they merged once again into the fog. Their fading calls seemed to say "follow us — follow us". When I grew older, I did follow and live with them.

I live in the country now, where I seldom see geese. But when they do fly overhead, their calls always tempt me to follow them again.

Children are especially aware of their kinship with animals. (Their pets, teddy bears, and animal books and pictures testify to this.) Any child will tell you that the most important part of a nature outing is seeing wild animals. The games in this chapter are designed to teach children simple and well-tested methods for attracting animals.

A.
B. Attracting birds, patience
C. Day and night/ thicket, forest
D. 1 or more
E. 4 years and up
F. None

BIRD-watchers have for years been thought of as rather strange eccentric types who trudge about the woods and climb trees with unruly collections of notebooks, binoculars and cameras. But if you ever get a chance to observe birds closely, you'll discover that they're beautiful to see and listen to, and utterly fascinating in their habits. You may find yourself not only understanding the bird-watcher's obsession, but catching it yourself!

In the bird world you'll find exquisite beauty and almost unimaginable ugliness, perfect grace and total clumsiness; fearsome power and gentle humility; silent soaring in rarified heights, and earthy cackling and squabbling.

There is a bird call that you can easily make with no more equipment than your own mouth. It attracts many of the smaller species: sparrows, warblers, jays, tits, nuthatches, flycatchers, wrens and several others. In the following section on predator calls, you will learn how to attract some of the larger birds.

The call consists of a series of rhythmically-repeated "psssh" sounds. Different rhythms work with different birds. Here are a couple of simple rhythms you can start with:

pssh . . . . . . pssh . . . . . . pssh . . . . . .
pssh . . . . . pssh . . . . . pssh-pssh . . . . . pssh . . . . . pssh

Each of these series should last about three seconds. Experiment to find the rhythms that work best for the birds in your area.

For the best results when you use this call, wait until you hear birds nearby, then kneel or stand motionless by shrubs or trees that will partially hide you and give the birds something to land on. Begin calling the series, pausing after three or four rounds to listen for incoming birds.

The birds will respond quickly if they are going to respond at all. Some birds will fly to the nearest lookout post to find out what is going on. Others will slowly, warily come closer. When the birds have come near, a single series or a couple of notes may be all you'll need to keep them nearby. I think the reason this call works is that the "pssh" sound resembles many birds' scolding call. (Some naturalists believe it sounds like a mother bird's feeding call to her young; others, that it merely provokes the birds' curiosity.)

Smaller birds dislike the presence of predators and will frequently mob a hawk or owl in hopes of driving it away. While hiking high in the mountains, a group of scouts and I experienced a dramatic case of bird-mobbing. We were in the middle of a low-growing alder thicket when a pine marten scampered into view just eight feet away. (Pine martens are related to the weasels and are about the size of a small domestic cat. They are agile climbers and snatch birds as part of their diet.)

We gave our "distress call", and in no more than a minute ten eager birds had gathered to rescue us. They landed very close to the marten, scolding him fervently and indignantly until he decided to move on.

Children enjoy using this call. Often I've been with groups of children who lay silently on the forest floor, completely absorbed in watching the birds that flew in overhead coming in answer to the children's signals.

Bird Calling

Birds on

THE INSPIRATION for this activity came from a statement I read or heard many years ago: "There are two kinds of bird-watchers. The first kind study birds at a distance, recording their physical characteristics and behaviour. The others are on more intimate terms with the birds; in fact, birds like them as much as they do other birds, and will even land on them to get as close to them as possible."

Not having Saint Francis' way with birds, but desiring a deeper rapport with the bird family, I wondered: would birds come to me if I added a few props to my bird-watching strategy? I'd used the "psssh" call for years, and had had birds almost land on my head. What would happen if I covered myself with a blanket and held a stick? Would birds land on the stick?

Not long ago I grabbed an old green blanket and an eight-foot branch and wandered through the forest until I heard bird calls. Sitting down and wrapping the blanket around me like a hooded robe, I held the stick motionless in the air and began making the "psssh" call. Immediately I heard approaching "aank-aank-aanks" and braced myself for the arrival of nuthatches. (Some kinds of nuthatches look rather like miniature woodpeckers.)

Out of the highest tree branches came two curious nuthatches. They paused to look around, so I called again, and one swooped down and landed on the tip of the branch I was holding. He began working his way down the branch until he was less than two feet from me, where he stared intently at my shadowed face. Meanwhile, the other nuthatch made the first of four trips from the nearest tree branch to my stick.

I've only used this camouflage ploy once myself; but

a Stick

A.
B. Attracting birds, patience
C. Day and night/ thicket, forest
D. 1 - 3 per group
E. 7 years and up
F. Drab-coloured blanket, stick

I've had two 12-year-old friends try it in the hope of getting a photograph of birds landing on their sticks. We haven't yet succeeded, but numerous birds have often flown just over their sticks and landed nearby

These are some suggestions and considerations we've found important for success with Birds on a Stick: 1. Birds are most active in the morning. 2. Birds are less likely to shy away from drab-coloured blankets and sheets. (Remember to cover your face with shadows cast by the blanket.) 3. Birds are more likely to approach you in a thicket or forest, where your presence is less obtrusive. 4. Choose a place where you can hear sounds of bird activity. 5. Position yourself in a clearing, so that the birds will have no other place to land but on your stick. 6. Hold the stick motionless. (Younger children can hold on to a young tree as their stick.)

Calling Predators

PREDATORS are very wary creatures. You'll rarely see foxes, pine martens, buzzards, hawks or eagles unless you have the good fortune to stumble upon or successfully track down a nest or den site. But their impressive wild beauty and rarity make it all the more exciting when you do see them. You can buy a predator call for a few pounds at some gunsmiths' shops, and with it draw these animals to you. The call imitates the sound of a wounded rabbit and often attracts curious non-predators as well; deer may come around out of curiosity.

Find an area with signs of heavy animal activity (game trails and animal droppings, for example). Hide yourself in a thicket or other natural cover with a clearing around it. The reason for the clearing is so you'll see the approaching animal long before he sees you. A group of college students ignored this precaution once and had a good scare when a fox jumped right in among them!

To use the predator call, hold the middle of it between your thumb and index fingers. The little finger should close over the end. For the first third of the call, keep your little finger over the end to suppress the noise; then release the little finger, ring, and middle fingers to achieve a wailing sound. Do this in one smooth sequence.

A.
B. Attracting predators, patience
C. Dawn, dusk, night/ areas with suitable cover
D. 1 or more
E. 7 years and up
F. Predator call

It should make a scream or cry not unlike a baby's wail.

You want as many animals as possible to hear the call, but you also want to produce a realistic effect as the animals come closer; so give a couple of very loud series of calls to attract their attention, then gradually lower the volume until the calls are only a whisper. Keep a watchful eye out, because a fox could be sneaking towards you.

Predator-calling doesn't work every time, but the results can be spectacular. A scout group and I once watched a wild cat slither to within 60 feet of us. Another time, a deer responded to the call by running up and snorting at me. And I was with another scout group when a large hawk screamed over our heads like a bullet, and disappeared from view. We then spotted a smaller bird circling overhead, so we forgot all about the hawk. Little did we know that he had landed quietly and was stalking us from behind; one of the scouts moved suddenly and startled the hawk into flight, just thirty-five feet behind us.

Children generally stay quiet and attentive during the half-hour I allow for calling. Even if no predators or deer come close, they enjoy the suspense and the silence of the forest, the scuffling of the squirrels, and the many bird calls.

A.
B. Stalking, wildlife observation
C. Dawn, dusk, night/anywhere
D. 1 or more
E. 7 years and up
F. None

Recon–Hike

AFTER preparing for the hike, create an atmosphere of suspense that the children will enjoy, by addressing the group in a serious, conspiratorial tone: *"We are about to undertake a special mission. Our objective is to search the surrounding area thoroughly, missing nothing. We are to observe and remember all the physical features and life-forms. There have been signs of recent predator activity in this area, so it is important that we remain hidden and unseen."*

These are the suggested preparations for the Recon–Hike: 1. Wear only non-rustling clothing like wool or cotton. 2. Camouflage yourself by wearing clothes that match the colours of the area. 3. Darken your face and hands. 4. Put on quiet walking shoes or go barefoot.

Guidelines to follow during the hike: 1. Always try to stay under or near cover. 2. Move slowly, pausing every few steps to look around. 3. Avoid walking in the same direction as the wind, so your scent won't be carried ahead of you.

Camouflaged reconnaissance increases a child's awareness of his environment and strengthens his ability to describe what he sees. Because the children are very quiet and watchful, there is a good chance of seeing wildlife. I recall a group of four eleven year-old boys at an environmental education camp who would do virtually anything to see wild animals. In fact, this game was born of the inspiration of their enthusiasm.

The first day at camp, these four boys asked me how they could see more animals. Because they were also interested in Red Indians, I told them that Indian hunters used to fast for several days to reduce their body scent, so that the animals they hunted couldn't smell them. I never dreamed that the boys would take my offhand comment seriously, much less that they would take it even further, I believe, than any Indian ever did.

The next day while we were swimming, one of the boys got stuck in a sea of gooey clay. We all pitched in to help pull him out, and of course before long you could hardly tell us apart. One of the boys, who was thoroughly plastered with clay, jubilantly announced that the animals could now neither smell nor see us, because the mud covered up our human scent and camouflaged our bodies as well.

Perfecting our disguises with generous dollops of clay, we headed warily for cover and then stalked the woods in search of animals. It was midday, so most of the animals were inactive and hidden from sight; still, we had great fun: we would spot a promising clearing, then divide up and surround it. On signal, five brown mud-caked forms would pop up from behind rocks, trees, and grass-clumps, gazing intently for any movements.

After an hour or so the caked mud began to itch horribly; we hurried back toward the camp to shower. Just as we entered the hall of the main building, an excited teacher met us. The Board of Education had just arrived to inspect the camp and were — at that very moment — just inside the door. No matter how badly we itched, we would simply have to wait out in the woods until they left. Our wait was sheer agony, but was relieved by many peals of boyish laughter.

ADVENTURES

By protecting ourselves from weather and soil, insects and animals, most of us have denied ourselves the vitality and sense of wellbeing that comes from being tuned into natural cycles and events. Our natural instinct for self-protection needs balancing by an adventurous spirit. A spirit of reaching-out to touch and explore the world places us where nature can easily demonstrate her powers to us.

At some time during my education as a naturalist, I heard that a certain Indian tribe used to hunt ducks by wading in the marshes at night. Under cover of darkness they walked right up to the ducks. As a bird-watcher, I was intrigued by the possibilities — I was eager to try observing waterfowl while immersed in the surrounding water.

*One evening I put on a pair of old trousers
and shoes and walked out to my favourite marsh.
As I neared the marsh around dusk, I was startled
by a thunderous roar. Thousands of geese
trembled together in a huge flock, flapping hard
to build momentum for takeoff ... then erupted,
covering the sky with their bodies. And skim-
ming over the reeds far ahead were countless
flocks of ducks, criss-crossing in every direction.*

*I hurried into the water, oblivious of its win-
try cold because of my awareness of the intense
energy of the marsh, vibrating through the forms
of fast-flying ducks and V-shaped signs of clam-
ouring geese. When the moonless night fell and
blended my presence into its darkness, the ducks
began flying extremely close. Whirs, wuffles, and
whistles passed by my ears — exhilarating! — and
ducks were alighting all around me like big
splashing raindrops.*

*Suddenly I sensed a presence overhead and
looked up; hovering right there above me was a
huge owl. With only my head out of the water,*

she couldn't decide whether I was fit prey or not. Meanwhile, ducks were paddling all around me, many coming so close I could have reached out and touched them. Later, when I was standing motionless in shallower water, one little duck swam unconcernedly between my legs.

The whole experience was so magical that I completely forgot myself and the cold. I spent two or three hours wading silently from one duck-inhabited pool to another, using my hands and ears to help to guide me through the night blackness.

It is very helpful — almost essential — for people to start with unusual, captivating experiences in nature. This kind of first contact extinguishes for a moment the self-enclosing preoccupations and worries that keep us from feeling at one with other forms of life. From that release into expanded awareness and concern, love naturally follows. And memories of moments of expansion and love of nature act as reminders of, and incentives to, a more sensitive way of living.

Still Hunting

STILL-HUNTING was practised by the American Indians. A brave who wanted to still-hunt would go to a place he knew well and felt attracted to. There, in the forest or on a hillside, he would sit down and let his mind settle into a still and watchful mood. If his arrival had caused a disturbance among the creatures around him, he waited patiently until the world of nature returned to its normal, harmonious routine. Usually, his only desire in still-hunting was to observe and to learn.

When you go still-hunting, let your sitting-place

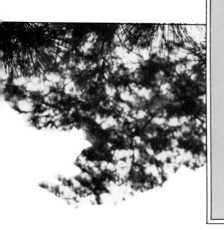

A.
B. Serenity, spotting wildlife
C. Day and night/any-where
D. 1 or more
E. 7 years and up
F. None

choose you. You may be intuitively guided to a specific place in order to learn a certain lesson. For the first part of your stay remain motionless, not even turning your head. Be as unobtrusive as you can, letting the world around you go on as it does when you aren't there. Feel that you are part of the natural surroundings; mentally move with the shimmering leaves, or dance with the butterfly as it darts and dodges through the air. Because you are still, curious animals may come close for a look at you. I was once approached from behind by a mysterious animal that made strange p-thumping noises as it moved. When the beast had come to within about seven feet, my courage flagged and I quickly turned my head. Off into the bushes fled that vicious predator, a startled rabbit!

Sharing private experiences with friends after a still-hunt brings a group closer together. Each still-hunter can tell about a plant or animal he has seen, and the way he felt about it. Another good way to share still-hunting experiences is for each child to act out for the others something he saw, or a feeling he had, while sitting. The others try to tune in to the deeper mood of each person. The tone of these sharing times should always be respectful and sensitive, if real communication of feelings and experiences is to happen.

A
B. Overcoming fears, night life
C. Dusk to night/ anywhere
D. 1 or more
E. 4 years and up
F. Torch (optional)

The
Night

BARKING DOGS, scratching noises, ghostly owl calls — at night, strange sounds deepen the mystery of the unknown world of the outdoors.

Many of the animals that can be heard at night are seldom seen — owls, badgers and foxes, for example. To increase your chances of spotting them, bring a torch to scan open clearings for their "eye shine". Hold the light near your eyes (on your forehead or nose). If you want to see them without having them see you, put a red filter or a piece of red cellophane over your torch

World

lens, since animals can't see red light.

Night hiking has other benefits besides the attraction of seeing nocturnal animals. Children are more reflective and communicative at night; I've noticed that as night falls a group of children will draw closer together for mutual support. After listening to the night sounds for awhile, their conversation begins to turn to fears of the dark and of wild animals. Often, discussion of their fears helps release them, and leaves everyone feeling relaxed and confident as we head back towards camp.

Survival Hike

"IF I GOT LOST out here, how would I stay alive?"
Everyone who has walked in wild places has imagined
himself lost and alone, without gear or food. What would
your chances of survival be, if it was just you and wilderness? To answer this question, take stock of how well
you actually know the outdoors. Surviving in the wild is
primarily a matter of familiarity with nature, and of
taking care of ourselves by making intelligent use of
what nature provides. The American Indian was able to
live close to nature for countless centuries because he
knew nature. He never dreaded being alone with the
elements, but positively enjoyed the experience.

Knowing the skills of survival gives us a confidence
and ease that help us to feel the innate bonds between
ourselves and the world.

Survival outings can be a lot of fun. They contain a
built-in element of adventure, even when they last for
only a few hours. As you become more and more skilled,
you may want to test your abilities by going out for
several days or a week at a time.

A good project for the initial outing is to learn how
to construct a shelter from natural materials. Fort-build-
ing is a passion of childhood, and the surprising ingenuity
and industry that children display can easily be tapped
with the help of your informed suggestions.

The site of the shelter is important. If you build care-
lessly, you may find that what you thought was a cosy
little hollow is actually a river bed, when sudden rains
bring a stream of water flowing cheerily through your
front room. Here are some suggestions for building a dry,
comfortable hut:

1. Build the shelter where it will receive the early
morning sun (dawn is the coldest part of the day), and

A.
B. Living with nature
C. Day and night/ anywhere
D. 1 or more
E. 9 years and up
F. Basic equipment

where it will be shaded from the hot afternoon sun in summer. 2. Avoid building your shelter under a canopy of evergreen leaves, as they will drip for hours after a snow or a rainstorm. 3. Build close to water and fuel (e.g., wood, or animal dung). 4. Find a breezy area, where there will be fewer midges in summer. 5. Don't build in a dry stream bed. 6. Make the shelter, or some ground signal that you've constructed visible to searchers.

Be sure to use only dead materials in your practice sessions; there's no good excuse for desecrating the landscape except in an emergency.

Themes for subsequent hikes could be: finding water and fuel, building and lighting fires, finding and preparing wild food, making equipment from natural materials, building various types of shelter, signalling for help, keeping warm and preventing hypothermia, using a compass and finding help, staying calm when lost. You'll find much helpful discussion of these subjects in these two books on survival: *The Spurbook of Survival and Rescue* by Terry Brown and Rob Hunter, an inexpensive book published by Spurbooks; a more detailed book is *The Outdoor Survival Handbook* by David Platten, published by David and Charles. For specific aspects of survival there are several useful books: Penguin publish *First Aid for Hill Walkers and Climbers* by Jane Renouf and Stewart Hulse; Fontana publish a guide to the edible wild plants of Britain, *Food for Free* by Richard Mabey; and Spurbooks publish a series of books on outdoor skills and safety including *Weather Lore* and *Map and Compass*.

Expanding

A.
B. Experiencing and appreciating nature
C. Day and night/anywhere
D. One
E. 10 years and up
F. None

ALL OF US have experienced an expanded sense of freedom at times — when our awareness went out to include more of the surrounding life as part of ourselves. At such times, our spirits rise with the soaring seagull tilting and swaying high above. The wind may seem to breathe life into every passing tree; a frightened covey of quail explodes in flight, leaving our bodies trembling with a nervous thrill; or the steady roar of a swollen mountain stream, tumbling through the rocks, calms us and takes our thoughts high over the mountains.

John Muir, a Scottish born naturalist who established several of the USA's best known national parks, would sometimes become so engrossed in his wanderings that a one-day outing would become a trek lasting several days or even weeks. And in his wanderings he had none of the "essential" supplies like food, warm clothing, or even sleeping bags. He was sustained by his love of beauty and solitude. Listen to his description of the inspiration that kept him going in wild places:

"Walk away quietly in any direction and taste the freedom of the mountaineer. . . . Climb the mountains and get their good tidings. Nature's peace will flow into you as sunshine flows into trees. The winds will blow their own freshness into you, and the storms their energies, while cares will drop off like autumn leaves."

I have come to realize that when, like John Muir, we enter the world of nature in a spirit of openness, splendid experiences come to us unsought. Receptivity enables us to feel invigorated, relaxed and inspired.

A special activity

SILENT
SHARING
WALK

OF ALL the activities in this book, the Silent Sharing Walk is potentially the most powerful. Walk in silence, abandoning words and the trappings of civilization — shoes, for example, and synthetic clothing that makes such un-nature-like noises. The silence and harmony of this activity, especially at dawn or dusk, create an awareness that we are sharing the world with all living things.

Animals can sense the state of mind of a group of humans; they won't run away if they feel you are relaxed and have peaceful intentions. (Deer seem especially sensitive in this way.) Often I've noticed, on these walks, how animals will move away from us without the frantic fear so common at the approach of human beings; instead, they retreat a few steps at a time, stopping to look over their shoulders and satisfy their curiosity. It's wonderful to sense our kinship with the animals, we enter their world as co-members, rather than as outsiders, and nature accepts us as part of itself.

Because the walk requires sensitivity and subtle appreciation, I offer it only to children who I feel will be receptive and able to enter into the spirit of silent sharing.

In a tall forest in the mountains, twelve boys and I prepared for a Silent Sharing Walk by remaining alone and apart for half an hour, in total silence. We then walked slowly down an old road that was overgrown and shaded by trees, towards a viewpoint where we would see the great valleys and plains, stretching out, far below. Birds and insects sang a chorus, and the air seemed electrified by our silence. A boy would spot something and tap the shoulders of his companions, pointing to whatever had caught his attention. The boys' eyes testified to feelings of calmness and joy.

We saw a doe moving slowly toward us, intent on

browsing in the undergrowth. When we were only 30 feet away, she gracefully raised her head and looked us over quietly. Her eyes were so innocent and trusting that they melted our hearts; rarely had we been accepted so unquestioningly into nature as now, by this gentle representative. There was an indescribable feeling about the moment — like coming home after a long exile.

Other shy animals which we would normally not see at all, stopped to watch us, curious about the silent strangers.

We arrived at the viewpoint overlooking the plain and stayed there for an hour, still in silence, letting ourselves be absorbed into the darkening wilderness.

When a person feels a sense of unity with the world, his feelings of harmony with other people are intensified, too. Through watching nature in silence, we discover within ourselves feelings of relatedness with whatever we see — plants, animals, stones, earth and sky.

The American Indians knew that, in silence, men can feel that all things are expressions of a single life, and that we humans, too, are children of that life. "As above, so below. As within, so without." As we get closer to nature, we find that the subject of our study is not actually nature at all, but life, and the nature of our own selves.

Unendingly magnificent is nature; yet we view only one of her billions of planets. Her splendour is spread across endless space and manifested on countless worlds; but, for us her most wonderful gift remains her willingness to teach us about ourselves. And when we learn to see and understand ourselves and the world around us, we humans become the pinnacle of nature's accomplishments; for through man, nature is able to view and appreciate itself in the fullest, most vividly aware way of all.

FROM HIS EARLIEST years Joseph Bharat Cornell has been sensitive to the mysteries and beauties of nature. As a boy he spent much time walking in the mountains.

Joseph designed his own BA degree course in nature awareness at California State University, then trained as a naturalist with the National Audubon Society. During the past eleven years he has taught in county schools in an outdoor education programme and he has also

worked as a naturalist for the Boy Scouts of America. During this period he has led many workshops for teachers and youth leaders.

Joseph Cornell is currently director of Earth Sky, a non-profit environmental group dedicated to imparting an increasing awareness of the natural world. The organisation runs workshops for teachers, leaders and parents who want to share their love of nature with children.

About the Author

Credits

Elizabeth Ann Kelley – Covers, Endpapers, 4, 15, 22/23, 32/33, 40/41, 52, 56/57, 58/59, 61, 69, 70/71, 76/77, 81, 92, 96/97, 101, 106/107, 114/115, 128/129, 134/135, 139

Bill Oetinger – Title page

Judy Daniel – 45

Dharani Dass – 86

Dalton Exley – 9, 66

Lincoln Exley – 6, 88

Photographs:

Joseph Bharat Cornell – 21, 54/55, 74/75, 83, 91, 103

John Hendrickson – 25, 28, 38/39, 41, 104/105, 112/113

George Beinhorn – Back Cover, 72/73, 94/95, 124/125 126/127,

Susan Landor – 46/47

Colin Campbell – 27

Raghunath Polden – 120/121, 130

Photographers unknown – 10, 138

Acknowledgements

THIS BOOK, like an oak tree, has drawn nourishment from many sources. I would particularly like to thank these friends who, by their suggestions, encouragement, and support helped make this book possible.

James Fuller. A professional youth leader, he first suggested writing this book, and has lent his continued support to the project.

Kathe Goria, John Hendrickson, Dick Paterson. Many ideas and inspirations in the book came from years of fruitful association with these friends and naturalists.

Garth Gilchrist. Much of Garth is contained within these pages. I am indebted to him also for arranging a secluded and inspiring three-week stay on a houseboat in the Klamath Marsh, during which we were able to work without distractions — except for sightings of uncommon birds and mammals.

George Beinhorn, Michael Deranja, Nancy Estep, Jean Rodgers, Asha Savage, and my other friends at Ananda Publications, for their helpful expertise.

I. Animals and Plants Speak Out

MANY PEOPLE judge the value of a plant or animal solely by the way it affects man. But all plants and animals make important contributions to their fellow life forms, thereby benefiting the entire cycle of life. The riddles below help us to understand how the animals and plants that we normally might consider pests actually contribute to the welfare of the whole.

Below each riddle you will see a row of letters. To decode the answer, write down, for each letter in the line, the letter that follows it in the alphabet.

Example: B N V = C O W.

Riddles:

I do my part to control the rodent population. This greatly benefits the plant world and helps the farmer, too. Nevertheless, most of you humans don't like me and fear me. What you don't realize is that I'm just as afraid of you as you are of me. Did you know that a five year old boy died of my bite in 1975. That was the first death in the UK for thirty years. Most of us are quite harmless. If I think you're about to step on me, I'll let you know where I am.

R M Z J D

Although I'm shy, I'm very patient in my work, and I can be quite creative. I work seasonally outdoors, but year-round indoors. I work hard to clean your house of nasty pests, but I don't like it when I'm mistaken for one of those pests myself! If it weren't for the few cousins who give us a bad name, humans would have greater respect and appreciation for our honourable family.

R O H C D Q

Most people don't like me because they think I'm slimy and rather disgusting. You certainly don't begin to understand that I'm really very important. Over a million of us live in every acre of grassland. We're like a permanent army of little ground diggers that keep your lawns green and make your land fertile. We aerate the soil. We keep it in good condition by breaking it up and mixing in plant material. We bring mineral rich soil to the surface. Without us your garden and fields would not look lush and green.

D Z Q S G V N Q L

At best you think of me as a persistant weed. Worse I sting you and give you a painful rash. I have many minute hairs which penetrate your skin, break off and inject a poisonous liquid into the wounds. But I'm very important for the well-being of some other plants and animals. I make the soil better so that other plants grow well. Many beautiful, rare kinds of butterflies lay their eggs on my leaves and feed on me. Butterfly breeders even grow acres of us! I am used for poultry and cattle fodder and make good compost. Your kind uses me by making a lotion to soothe the rash I cause or to treat burns. I'm used for setting junket and for making linen, paper and twine. I'm even eaten by some of you and in times of trouble you may want to collect me instead of destroying me. That is because my young leaves have lots of iron and vitamin C. In the first world war thousands of tons of us were collected for a camouflage dye.

M D S S K D

You hate me and most of my 85,000 kinds of relations. My relations sting you, spread sleeping sickness, yellow fever, malaria, plague and many other kinds of disease. I myself am such a vicious little horror that in the Western Highlands I have been accused (along with the kilt) of causing the Highland fling. If you stay late on a picnic or camp, you'll know who I am. Millions of us will drive you mad and sting you. But all my kind are a vital part of the food chain. Without us there wouldn't be as many animals inhabiting the sky and water as there are now. And the fishermen who curse us would not catch so many fish.

L H C F D

You probably think of us as being dirty and spreading disease. True. We're quite capable of killing you. Even if you let us multiply in your kitchen we can give you a nasty stomach upset. But the living world needs us. Without us water would be dirty. Nothing would rot so that plants would not grow: they would get no food from the soil. Then animals would have nothing to eat. They would die and so would you. Your kind also need us to tan leather, to treat sewage and to prepare linen from flax. We're vital when you make vinegar, wine, cheese or yoghurt. No matter how you fear us you wouldn't exist without us!

A Z B S D Q H Z

II. Animal Game Clues

1. I move quickly now, but not so in my youth.
2. I usually hunt near water.
3. I eat flying insects.
4. I'm a strong flier.
5. Sometimes I'm very colourful.
6. I'm cold-blooded and I wear my skeleton on the outside instead of the inside.
7. I have two more legs than a mouse and have very large eyes.
8. With my four wings I look like a helicopter flying in the air.

C Q Z F N M E K X

1. I will eat anything that moves and can be swallowed.
2. I hibernate in winter, except where it is warm.
3. I must live in damp or wet places, avoiding the dry heat of summer and the cold of winter.
4. Almost all my kin lay their eggs in water.
5. I'm chunky and wouldn't win very many races.
6. Almost all my kin sing.
7. I can secrete a sticky white poison. In some of my kin this poison can kill or paralyze dogs and other predators who might try to eat them.
8. My close kin travel farther away from water than our distant cousins whom you might be thinking of. Also, it isn't true, as some say, that I will give you warts.

S N Z C

1. I can walk and swim.
2. My vision is good, but I don't have a good sense of smell.
3. I care for and raise my young.
4. My body temperature stays the same.
5. My kind are very adaptable and live in many different environments.

6. I like to change my environment.
7. I walk on two feet and speak several different languages.

G T L Z M

1. My body temperature is usually seven degrees warmer than man's.
2. Each foot of mine has two toes in front and two at the back. I can run up trees and I'm a bit like an acrobatic steeplejack.
3. I have a tongue three times as long as my bill. It is about 10 centimetres long and can get frostbite if I don't fly to a warm area in winter.
4. My stiff spiny tail feathers act as a prop when I hunt for my food.
5. My diet consists mainly of tree-boring insects, but also of ants, acorns, flying insects, berries, and sap.
6. My nest is a cavity in a tree that I make myself.
7. My bill is used for chiselling wood. I am best known for the drumming noise I make, which can be heard a quarter of a mile away on a quiet day.

V N N C O D B J D Q

1. I am nine inches long.
2. I build a large leafy nest by a hedge or wall.
3. When I'm an adult I live alone.
4. I live in the countryside or in the suburbs.
5. I am nocturnal, but you may see me after it rains.
6. The cold is my worst enemy, then it's motor cars. Animals don't harm me.
7. I eat mostly grubs, snails, earthworms and insects. I'll eat a dead mouse or sparrow if I find one.
8. I hibernate, so I eat a lot in autumn.
9. Humans like me but don't keep me as a pet — mainly because I'm covered in fleas. Incidentally, my kind of fleas can't live on you and don't even like biting you. I must admit they'll make you itch.

10. I protect myself by rolling in a prickly ball.
G D C F D G N F

1. I am usually nocturnal.
2. I have a rich, dark brown, thick fur, and a bushy tail.
3. I do not hibernate.
4. I can run very fast indeed. I climb very well and jump easily from branch to branch.
5. I am about two and a half feet long.
6. I used to be very common but now I am rare. Today I live in Scotland, North Wales and the Lake District.
7. I used to be trapped for my lovely fur. These days my main killer is still traps — usually set for ferrets or foxes.
8. You may not even know my name but it includes a favourite tree.

O H M D   L Z Q S D M

1. I am equally as happy living on the bleak moorland as in the city centre.
2. In the 1950's and 1960's my kind died in their thousands because of chemicals used in agriculture. Later these were banned.
3. Today I am certainly not an endangered species. There are over 100,000 breeding pairs of my kind in the UK alone.

4. I am a predator.
5. I nest in pylons, telegraph poles, tall tower blocks, cliff ledges or tall trees. I have been known to nest on a crane, Nelson's column and Westminster Abbey.

6. I hover up to fifty feet above the ground and then drop down on my victim.
7. Watch for me at dusk on the M6, M4 and M1. My favourite hunting grounds are the uncut verges of motorways where I find my tastiest victim, the vole.
8. I am a member of the falcon family and my name begins with a K.

J D R S Q D K

1. I usually come out at night to eat, and I leave old bones and feathers behind. In fact, I'm untidy and a bit smelly.
2. I hide or bury my food under the ground for eating another day.
3. I often live in a rabbit's burrow, a badger set or under tree roots, but I'm just as happy under a garden shed. Both town and country suit me well.
4. I like to eat frogs, rabbits and sometimes baby lambs. A duck or goose is a special treat. I'm a bit of a scavenger and will find food in compost heaps, litter bins and on bird tables.
5. My enemies are human hunters and dogs.
6. My fur is reddish brown but I have a patch of white fur on my throat.
7. I have yellow eyes. Maybe it's these that give humans the idea that I'm a bit sly and cunning. Actually I'm intelligent, quick and I take risks. I must admit I'm a bit of an opportunist.
8. I have a long bushy tail, with a white tip. It is called a brush.

E N W

1. I am one of your favourite friends.
2. You think of me as friendly and tame but I am very aggressive if any of my own kind venture on to my territory. We fight fiercely.

3. I court my female by feeding her.
4. I love gardens, especially when you dig.
5. Earthworms and insects are my favourite foods.
6. I make my nest of moss, grass and hair.
7. My song is sweet. You can hear me on more days a year than any of my relations anywhere in Europe.
8. I brighten your winter garden.
9. The young of my kind are brown and speckled but both parents have a colourful breast.
10. My picture appears on many of your Christmas cards.

Q N A H M

1. If you want to find me, look for water.
2. I'm a carnivore and eat mostly insects, and the smaller of my kind.
3. I am a fast, strong swimmer.
4. I need cold, well-oxygenated water to live in.
5. I spawn my eggs during the spring, in small clear streams.
6. I'm slim and sleek.
7. I'm as pretty as a rainbow.

Q Z H M A N V   S Q N T S

1. I have four distinct stages in my life-cycle.
2. I am a good pollinator.
3. Your parents may not want me near their vegetable plants. (Tell them to plant nasturtiums to keep me better fed.)
4. I am one of the worst sufferers from the destruction of the environment and poisonous chemicals. Many of my kind are threatened or gone forever. Please don't cut your motorway verges, pull up hedges or use poisonous weedkillers.
5. You don't think much of me in the third stage of my life-cycle but as an adult, many people think I'm

the most colourful and beautiful of all nature's fauna.
6. We are given pretty names like Tortoiseshell, Swallow-tail, Peacock and Red Admiral.

A T S S D Q E K X

1. I am very shy.
2. I am most active at night and rest during the day.
3. My feet are webbed.
4. My enemy is man and his pollution. Fishermen and the American mink kill me.
5. Even though I'm a wonderful swimmer, I can trot and gallop as well.
6. If you hear a musical whistle it could be me.
7. To me the tastiest foods are eels, salmon and trout. I also eat other fish, birds, frogs, crayfish, voles and rabbits.
8. My teeth are very sharp and I can easily nip off one of your fingers.
9. I make slides and I love to career down into the water. In summer I make mud slides and in winter I make snow slides. I can play for hours on end.

N S S D Q

Other interesting Exley books for young people

Free Stuff for Kids. Over a hundred different things children can write for from British manufacturers. All are free or cost less than £2. Badges and buttons, books and booklets, games, stamps, posters, – it's an almost endless list, and immense fun. Children can learn how to write their own letters and can find out how to use the post to pursue their own interests. £2.95

What it's like to be Me. An outstanding collection of poems, prose and illustrations by disabled children all over the world. Basically the book will help parents and teachers to create an understanding of the real problems of the disabled. Children who are blind, deaf, or physically handicapped tell able-bodied children what it's like to be disabled, what their hopes and expectations are, and why, above all, they want to be accepted as fully integrated members of society. "Full of courage and wry humour, as you might expect. I like the book very much...eloquent testimony to the fact that disabled children passionately want to play their part in society as equals." (Lord Snowdon). £4.95

Discovering Nature. Polar bears and wild mountains are nature – but so, too, is a chicken skeleton, or apples rotting in a basket. This intriguing new book deliberately sets out to provide children with nature projects they can carry out in their own home or garden. No expensive equipment is needed, there's no need to travel, and there's as much fun for girls as for boys. In one experiment the children boil the chicken bones from the family dinner and re-create with nylon and wires the complexities of the skeleton. In another they create patterns with mushroom spore. In yet another they make simple bird boxes and a tree house observation hide. The book is illustrated with many colour and black and white illustrations. £4.95 paperback.

Cry for our Beautiful World. This book has been created by children passionately concerned about the preservation of wildlife. Children from Peking tell the story of the Giant Panda in its natural surroundings. Children from Tanzania write about the conflict between human and wildlife priorities. Children from India describe the threat to the tiger. And children throughout the western world talk about their fears of pollution, and their conviction that there may be a way to balance man's needs with those of the world he lives in. A deeply moving book that deserves a very wide audience. Many beautiful colour pictures. £9.95

Julius. Children love this story. Julius, a baby chimpanzee, was born at Christmas in Kristiansand Zoo, Norway. At six weeks he was abandoned by his mother, bitten and injured. He was 'adopted' by two human families, who knew that one day they would face heartbreak – for he would eventually have to return to the other chimps. Julius grows quickly, is mischievous and very lovable. He's into everything, the fridge, the children's toys. Gradually – and very frightened at first – he is re-introduced to the other chimps, then he spends a last Christmas with his human friends. £5.95 hardback

Order through your bookshop, or by post from Exley Publications Ltd, 16 Chalk Hill, Watford WD1 4BN. Please add £1 per book (maximum £2) to cover postage and packing.

52 379 518 3

K — 11 — 18
21/3

HIT

Please renew or return items by the date
shown on your receipt

www.hertfordshire.gov.uk/libraries

Renewals and enquiries: 0300 123 4049

Textphone for hearing or   0300 123 4041
speech impaired users:

L32 11.16

Hertfordshire